Causal Models

Causal Models

How People Think about the World and Its Alternatives

Steven Sloman

OXFORD
UNIVERSITY PRESS
2005

OXFORD
UNIVERSITY PRESS

Oxford University Press, Inc., publishes works that further
Oxford University's objective of excellence
in research, scholarship, and education.

Oxford   New York
Auckland   Cape Town   Dar es Salaam   Hong Kong   Karachi
Kuala Lumpur   Madrid   Melbourne   Mexico City   Nairobi
New Delhi   Shanghai   Taipei   Toronto

With offices in
Argentina   Austria   Brazil   Chile   Czech Republic   France   Greece
Guatemala   Hungary   Italy   Japan   Poland   Portugal   Singapore
South Korea   Switzerland   Thailand   Turkey   Ukraine   Vietnam

Copyright © 2005 by Oxford University Press, Inc.

Published by Oxford University Press, Inc.
198 Madison Avenue, New York, New York 10016

www.oup.com

Oxford is a registered trademark of Oxford University Press

Library of Congress Cataloging-in-Publication Data
Sloman, Steven A.
Causal models : how people think about the world and its alternatives /
by Steven Sloman.
p.   cm.
Includes bibliographical references and index.
ISBN-13 978-0-19-518311-5
ISBN 0-19-518311-8
1. Psychology—Mathematical models.   2. Causation.   I. Title.
BF39.S56 2005
122—dc22   2004031000

2 4 6 8 9 7 5 3 1

Printed in the United States of America
on acid-free paper

To my ultimate causes: Linda, Sabina, Leila

Acknowledgments

When people think and learn, they're often thinking and learning about the way the world works. This simple truism forces those of us who study how people think and learn to worry about causality. A lot. This has not gone unappreciated. Any area of the study of cognition will either have been asking questions about causality for a long time (usually with some futility) or be actively avoiding such questions (deferring them for "future research"). The problem, I think, is that until recently no one has been able to frame the problem; the discussion of causality was largely based on a framework developed in the 18th century.

But that's changed. Great new ideas about how to represent causal systems and how to learn and reason about them have been developed by philosophers, statisticians, and computer scientists. The key insight is that causal reasoning is really about the logic of intervention, an insight carried into modern discourse in cognitive science, philosophy, and statistics by Peter Spirtes, Clark Glymour, and Richard Scheines's book *Causation, Prediction, and Search*, first published in 1993. I needed another book, though, to explain to me what the first book was talking about and to draw out some of its implications, *Causality* by Judea Pearl. My book would not have been written without either of the previous two. Of course, none of those authors is responsible for anything I say in this book; indeed, there may be little in it that they'd want to endorse. My aim is to give a very simple (and simplified) introduction to their ideas, while reviewing some of the work in cognitive science and psychology showing the manifestations of causal thinking.

This book is to some extent an exposition of conversations with Dave Lagnado, who spent a year working with me at my home institution, Brown University. Though the time was brief, it was a period of intense discussion and new understanding on my part. It has also benefited from the depth and breadth of knowledge consistently offered by York Hagmayer, along with his thoughtfulness and cooking.

Valuable comments on style and content have been provided by my wife, Linda Covington, by my sister, Heather Sloman, by the piercing intelligence of Michelle Cowley, and by Caren Frosch. David Danks provided a penetrating critique of the manuscript that helped me correct some of my more serious blunders. The book also benefited from comments by Bob Rehder and several anonymous reviewers. Amy Brand was a regular fount of valuable advice for circumnavigating the complicated world of publishing.

Like all books, this one reflects the thinking of many people. To name only the most salient, I've profited from discussions about causality with Josh Tenenbaum, Clark Glymour, Michael Waldmann, and Dave Sobel. My thinking about issues discussed in this book has been shaped by conversations with Lance Rips, David Over, Barbara Malt, Constantinos Hadjichristidis, Larry Barsalou, Sergio Chaigneau, Bill Warren, Julie Sedivy, Andy Horwitz, and Denis Hilton.

Finally, I'd like to thank some of the students whose labor is hidden in these pages: Daniel Mochon, Ian Lyons, Henry Parkin, and Daniel Acheson. Marianne Harrison is responsible for the figures.

Much of the research reported was funded by a grant from NASA (NCC2-1217). A good chunk of the writing was done while I was visiting the Laboratoire de Psychologie Cognitive, Université de Provence, Aix-en-Provence, France. It wouldn't have been possible without the support there of Jonathan Grainger and Aline Pelissier.

And, of course, there are my other root causes, my parents, Valerie and Leon. I am merely an effect.

Contents

Part II. Evidence and Application

Causal Models

1

Agency and the Role of Causation in Mental Life

The High Church of Cognitive Science: A Heretical View

How do people think? The effort to answer this question is the domain of cognitive science, a field of study that includes cognitive psychology and parts of computer science, linguistics, anthropology, and philosophy. The field emerged in lock-step with the development of the computer. After all, the computer is at heart an information-processing device, and it would seem that people are information-processing devices extraordinaire. Computers have input devices (e.g., keyboards, mouses, microphones), and people have input devices (e.g., eyes, ears, skin). Computers store information in memories; people store information in memories. Computers compute; they do calculations by transforming symbols in languages they understand (like Java and binary code); people compute by transforming symbols in languages that we understand (like English and arithmetic). Computers have output devices (e.g., screens, speakers, disk drives), and people have output devices (e.g., mouths, hands, feet). Indeed, it would seem, and it did seem for many years (it still does to some), that cognitive science would answer the question "how do people think?" by programming a computer to behave like a person. The program would be the answer. This was essentially the conclusion offered by Alan Turing in a famous essay called "Computing Machinery and Intelligence."[1] He carefully

3

developed a clever way known as the Turing Test to decide if a computer could think by fooling a judge into believing that it was a man and not a woman.

Now there are contests modeled on the Turing Test. The Loebner Prize offers a gold medal and $100,000 for the first computer whose responses are indistinguishable from a human's. Each year an annual prize of $2000 and a bronze medal is awarded to the most human computer. Some machines have proven very clever, but nobody has built a machine that can come close to passing the test as Turing envisioned it. Nobody has yet won gold. One reason may be the complexity of thought or the huge amount of knowledge required to mimic even a young child. Think about how much knowledge is required to understand something as simple as a chair. You need to understand sitting (and that requires knowledge about the human form). You need to understand something about materials (chairs cannot be made out of powdered sugar). You can't even really understand what a chair is without understanding something about fatigue, the benefits of rest, and perhaps the importance and ritual of breakfast, lunch, and dinner. Knowledge is interrelated and therefore a critical mass is required even to understand the simplest things.

Disillusionment with the view that the computer is the best metaphor of mind, sometimes called the High Church Doctrine of Cognitive Science, has been widespread and has deep roots. People differ from computers in critical ways. For one, we compute differently. Traditionally, computers perform one operation at a time; they compute sequentially. People are able to perform many operations at a time; certain functions (like memory) involve the simultaneous operation of billions of simple units, resonating together to retrieve memories, in the way the entire body "remembers" how to ride a bike. Some recent computer designs involve a limited amount of parallel processing, but nothing like the parallelism that operates in the mind.

A second difference is that, unlike computers, people have emotional lives directly tied to the chemical composition and physiological processes of our bodies. We may be machines, but we're machines made out of meat, and that changes everything.

A third difference, and the one that I'm going to focus on, is that we're not passive consumers of information, blindly transforming symbols as requested. We're agents. We actively pursue goals, be they the need for food, oxygen, or love or the desire for entertainment, education, or liberty. Whether people have free will is a question far beyond the scope of this book. But it seems clear that we talk, think, and act as if we do. Therefore, to understand the mind requires a way of representing agency.

Agency Is the Ability to Represent Causal Intervention

Understanding what it means to be an agent may seem to require answers to questions like "what is consciousness?" "how is intentionality coded in the brain?" and "what does it mean to be aware?" But agency can be understood in much more mundane, yet comprehensible, terms. Agency can be treated as nothing more than the ability to intervene on the world and change it. And I'm not even going to claim that people have that ability, although they probably do.

All I'm going to claim is that people *represent* the ability to intervene in the world and change it. Think about human knowledge. What do you know? One kind of thing you know is how things work in the world. You know about mechanisms. You know how to operate some machines; you know the buttons to press, the levers to push. You know how it behaves (it hums, it rattles, it lights up, it glides). You have some ideas about what makes people go, their motivations and behaviors. You know Johnny is driven by his stomach and Nancy by her pride. You know about the mechanisms that drive political systems, about power and economics.

This knowledge is all causal in the sense that it's about the mechanisms that bring about effects from causes. It's all about events that take place in time and describes not only how and when objects and events appear together but why. The answer to this why question comes in the form of descriptions of how things could be otherwise, not only which effects follow which causes but which effects would follow if the causes had been different. As the 18th century Scottish philosopher David Hume put it, causality is about "an object followed by another, . . . where, if the first had not existed, the second had never existed." This is precisely the kind of knowledge required to predict the effect of action, how behavior changes the world.

What do we really understand when we think we understand a mechanism? Presumably, at minimum, we have some idea about which inputs produce which outputs. We understand how the choice of inputs determines the outputs and that the reverse does not hold. The choice of outputs does not determine the value of inputs. This special and structured kind of knowledge requires that we understand that (1) changing X is likely to end up with a change in Y; (2) causes and effects are asymmetric: changing Y won't budge X; (3) causes and effects go together over time; and (4) Y does not occur before X. Believing that heat causes expansion requires believing that (1) changing the temperature will change the volume (of a gas, say); (2) changing the volume won't change the temperature; (3) certain temperatures are associated with certain volumes; and (4) new volumes aren't observed before new temperatures.

I'm defining knowledge as a set of beliefs about change in the world and the mechanisms that support those changes. Knowledge is about how changes in some things lead to changes in other things. In other words, what we know about the world is how things could have been otherwise. Representations of causality allow us to describe how the world would have been—that is, another possible world—if some cause had had a different value, for then its effects would have been different. In cognitive science, this is the domain of counterfactuals, beliefs/statements about worlds that are not necessarily this one, like the world in which today is a balmy 18°C, with a light breeze blowing off a sky-blue sea (fortunately, sometimes counterfactuals are about the world as it actually is).

So agency concerns intervention on the world to change it, to see how things might have been otherwise. But even more important, agency is about how we represent intervention, how we think about changes in the world. Because by being able to represent it, we are able to imagine changes in the world without actually changing it. And that ability opens up the possibility of imagination, fantasy, thinking about the future, thinking about what the past might have been like if only....

The Purpose of This Book

This book is about how to understand causal systems. But causal systems can't be understood without an analysis of cognition, for a causal claim is intrinsically a claim about beliefs, not merely a claim about the way the world is. Causality isn't just a figment of our imagination entirely independent of the actual world (if it were, then we'd be free to impose any causal relations we wanted, between, say, touching things and having them turn into gold). But causality is a form of construal. We impose a causal frame on the world to understand it, a frame that tells us about the mechanisms that not only produced the world as it is but that (counterfactually) govern the world however it had turned out.

Causal frames allow us to understand certain things (the mechanisms that take us from one state to another), including very important things like why people act the way they do and how to build an aqueduct. They may even be important for understanding why people are so often enamored of magic and where some religious belief comes from. This book will argue that they're critical for understanding how people reason and make judgments and decisions, certain aspects of language, and how we think about moral, legal, scientific issues and more. But they're not necessarily helpful for allowing us to understand noncausal formal systems like counting or other aspects of the way we represent the world, such as the images we use to try to remember the color of our front door or whether any of our high school teachers had a moustache.

The book was inspired in large part by the development in computer science, statistics, and philosophy of a general framework for representing causal relations, powerful enough to express the diversity of causal relations, whether probabilistic or deterministic, necessary or sufficient, weak or strong, direct or indirect, actual or background.[2] The framework is largely based on a mathematical framework for representing probability known as Bayesian networks. My plan is to discuss the developments mainly at a conceptual, not mathematical, level. For mathematical introductions, I refer readers to some excellent technical books.[3] What's unique about the causal model framework is that it gives us a way to think about the effect of action in the world. It makes the claim that the cognitive apparatus that people use to understand the world has a specialized operation that encodes certain changes in the world as the effect of agency, of intervention. These representations differ from other representations of change in being easily reversible. They invoke localized changes to causal models that are simple but have enormous effects. And what's so useful about them is not only that they give us a way to represent action but that they also give us a way to represent imagined action, how we think about the way the world could or would be if such and such were different.

The framework is extraordinarily rich but highly technical, though I'll discuss technical details only in a cursory way. What I'll do instead is to draw out the implications of the framework for cognition, what it says about how people reason, decide, judge, imagine, classify, talk, and how we learn to do all this in just a few short years of life. To foreshadow: in large part, we don't learn to do these things ourselves but depend very much on the people and institutions around us.

Plan of the Book

This book will be a long argument that causation is central in how humans understand the world. The first part will focus on the theory of causal models. Chapters 2 and 3 will provide a conceptual introduction to the significant ideas. Chapter 2 focuses on why cause matters and chapter 3 on what causes are. Chapters 4 and 5 provide the technical meat of the book; chapter 4 is about causal models generally, and chapter 5 is about the representation of intervention. Although I've tried to keep these chapters as light as possible, too light for more mathematically sophisticated readers, less technical readers are liable to find them hard going. The rest of the book can be read fruitfully without them. Nevertheless, I encourage all readers to struggle through them, because the excitement that ideas about causation and intervention have engendered in so many psychologists and other scientists, philosophers, and applied mathematicians can be shared only after having glimpsed the richness and detail of the ideas.

The second part of the book applies the theory to various domains of everyday life: how we reason (chapter 6); how we make decisions (chapter 7); how we judge (chapter 8); how we categorize objects (chapter 9); how we induce properties of the world (chapter 10); how we use aspects of language (chapter 11); and how we learn about causal structure and the strength of causal relations (chapter 12). These chapters are ordered according to how naturally they follow from the theoretical discussion of part I and how smoothly they follow one another. None of them is particularly difficult, but reading the earlier chapters first should make the later ones easier to fathom. But it may not, and the reader should feel free to pick and choose the chapters whose topics suit his or her fancy. Much of the scientific work on causal models has focused on learning. Because that topic is the most complex, I've left it to the end. Keep in mind that my intent is not to provide exhaustive surveys of each subfield but to give a sense of the central role that causal models play in each.

The final chapter, chapter 13, attempts to draw out the general lessons of causal and interventional principles for an understanding of people, their situations, their problems, and solutions to their problems.

I

THE THEORY

2

The Information Is in the Invariants

After locating food, a honeybee will return to its hive and perform an elaborate dance to signal the food's location to its cohort. Most bee experts believe, following Nobel Prize–winning work by Karl von Frisch, that a bee that has located a source of nectar more than about 100 yards away will return to the hive and repeat a figure eight pattern that includes a straight movement in which the bee waggles or vibrates its abdomen for a few seconds and then circles back first to one side and then to the other. The orientation of the straight movement relative to vertical tells the other bees the direction of the nectar relative to the sun; the duration of the waggles reveals the distance of the flower patch from the hive. The bee's dance focuses on only two critical elements for finding food; it presupposes that the only thing the other bees care about is the direction and distance to the food source. They don't care what the color of the terrain they'll be flying over is or whether it's made of rocks or sand. Neither of these things matters when a bee flies through the air to a flower patch. This example illustrates that animals are selective in what they attend to. They attend to the properties that serve their goals as best they can, while ignoring the properties that are irrelevant.

A useful skill for all moving organisms is the ability to predict how long it will take before an approaching object (like a wall) is bashed into. This is called time to collision. Being able to estimate time to collision can help one avoid obstacles when flying (if you're a bee or a pigeon), jumping (if you're a locust), or driving (if you're a human). It can also help you catch or hit a ball when it is the object that is moving and you are stationary. It turns out that when objects are neither speeding up or slowing down but moving at a constant velocity, time to collision can be estimated through an incredibly simple calculation based on the fact that the image of an object on your retina gets larger as you get closer to the object (or it gets closer to you). To estimate time to collision specifically, all you need to know is how big the image of the object is on your retina and how fast the size of the image is expanding. Divide the image size by its rate of expansion and that's it; that calculation gives you an excellent estimate of how long it will be before a big bang. This estimate is called tau (it was first derived in a science fiction novel by astronomer Fred Hoyle[1]). A fair amount of evidence suggests that locusts, birds, and people are all sensitive to tau when performing tasks that require estimates of collision time (like jumping out of the way of a looming entomologist, in the case of a locust). In fact, a type of neuron in locusts has been identified that is tightly tuned to the time to collision with an object approaching in a direct collision course.

Tau exemplifies how the environment can give us rich information in a simple form about something important. By ignoring almost everything about an object except the size of its image on the retina and how that image is changing, we render vital information immediately available for making contact (when catching) and avoiding contact (when navigating). Tau is so useful because it refers to a relation that doesn't change, that is *invariant*. The size of an image relative to its rate of expansion consistently indicates time to collision in many situations.

When learning to drive a car, a human being will appreciate that the steering wheel turns the wheels and that the brake will cause deceleration. They might notice the color of the upholstery, but they will also be aware that the color has no effect on the car's motion. When getting into a car they have not driven before, a person won't flinch in the face of new upholstery (even if it's green), but they'll be at a complete loss if there is no steering wheel. In this case, we have selective attention to invariants that reflect causal relations that we are aware of. We know that steering wheels cause changes in direction and brakes cause deceleration.

Taken together, these examples show three properties of behavior. First, animals are selective in what they attend to. Second, animals attend to what is stable—to invariants—because that's where the crucial information is for helping them achieve their goals. Third, at least for humans (and probably for other animals), invariants can take the form of causal relations. Causal relations carry the information that we store, that we discuss, and that we use for performing everyday activities that change the state of the world. Let's consider each of these three properties of behavior.

Selective Attention

The world is infinitely rich and complicated According to William James, babies experience the world "as one great blooming, buzzing confusion." James's contention would have been right, and would be applicable to adults, too, if perception didn't impose structure, so that we do not pay equal attention to every sensation and fact.

Imagine taking note of every fact around you at the moment, every shadow, every illuminated surface, every object, and the parts of each object. And then there are the relations among each of these things. Which surfaces are obstructing the view of which other surfaces? Which objects are supporting which other objects? What is the purpose of each object? Why is it there? If we took note of each of these things at every moment of every day, we'd collect enough information to fill several libraries every month. But who would care? What use would it serve anybody to take note of the fact that yesterday a dirty glass was beside the microwave and not the toaster before it was washed? Most facts are useless, and taking note of them would merely clog our minds.

The famous Russian psychologist Alexander Luria had a patient ("S") who had a fabulous memory.[2] He could reproduce a table of 50 digits after studying it for only 3 minutes. He could memorize long equations even though they made no sense to him, and he could memorize poetry in Italian, a language he did not speak. He could remember countless arbitrary facts based largely on a rare talent for constructing and maintaining vivid, detailed images from multiple senses: vision, audition, even taste. Yet he had trouble finding structure and meaning. Given a series of numbers that progressed in a simple logical order:

    1 2 3 4
    2 3 4 5
    3 4 5 6
    4 5 6 7,

he could reproduce the series yet not notice the logic of the sequence! Indeed, he would take as long to memorize a sequence like this as a sequence consisting of random digits. He complained that the vividness of the images that he evoked would clog his mind and make it hard for him to understand text and speech. The onslaught of images would confuse him and made it hard for him to maintain a job, except as a professional mnemonist in theaters. The ability to remember is useless without the ability to pick and choose what is important and to put the useful pieces together in meaningful ways.

Organisms must be selective; they must attend only to those things that carry the information relevant to their general interests and current goals to guide them through the world. A bee looking for nectar focuses on direction and distance from the hive, and a pigeon trying to avoid a tree focuses on the image of the tree and how fast it's expanding. Similarly, if you want to make friends and influence people, you should attend to their attitudes, behavioral responses, and their names. You can feel free to ignore how many freckles they have on their noses and, usually, whether they've passed through Toledo, Ohio. A person looking for entertainment would do well to head toward a stereo or bookshelf rather than the broom closet. Even the broom closet can be ignored from time to time.

Selective Attention Focuses on Invariants

So what do we select to attend to? Obviously, the answer is "it depends." If we're looking for shoes, we attend to shoe shops and if we're looking for hats, we attend to hat shops. More abstractly, we look for the places, the objects, the events, the information that will satisfy our current goals. We can think of selective attention as solving a problem. We want to get somewhere, to satisfy some desire or requirement, so we have to find those aspects of the environment that hold the solution so that we can limit our attention to them.

Generally, we know just what to do because we've done it before or because somebody tells us what to do. We already know how to start a car so we immediately attend to the location of the key, the brake, the accelerator pedal, and in some cars the clutch. We know how to purchase something in a department store, so we look for the cash register. And if we don't know these things (as we might not in a foreign country), we ask. In each case, what we need to know is something that holds not just in a single case but in all, or at least many, relevant cases. The great value in knowing about car keys and accelerator pedals is that so many cars have them. The utility of knowing about cash registers is that they have the power to give us ownership of a product in so many different stores.

We have a kind of expertise in car starting and consumerism that derives from knowing what *doesn't change* across instances and across time, that is, from knowing what's *invariant*.

Expertise inevitably involves the ability to identify invariants. Experts can do far more than list facts about their area of expertise. They can tell you what's important and what's more peripheral because they know what explains the way things are and they know what predicts the way things will be. An electrician focuses immediately on what's connected to what and how they're connected, ignoring whether the connection is visible or hidden behind walls; a plumber looks at the angle (or *fall*) of a pipe to make sure it's steep enough to allow water to flow but not so steep that the water will flow too fast, ignoring the design of the pipe manufacturer's trademark. A psychological counselor helping someone who is depressed will focus on the human relationships in that person's life, ignoring what their favorite color is.

In each case, the expert has picked out the properties that explain why the system (electrical, plumbing, or emotional) is in its current state and that predict the state of the system in the future. What allows the expert to do so is that these critical properties are the same from occasion to occasion. It's not the case that plumbing systems sometimes depend on the trademark design and sometimes on fall, and it's not the case that electrical circuits sometimes depend on how things are connected and sometimes don't. The properties that matter are invariant across situations and across individuals; otherwise, they wouldn't be learnable. So the knowledge that gives us expertise is knowledge about those aspects that are durable, that don't change with the wind, but that represent the stable, consistent, and reliable properties that hold across time and across different instantiations of a given system.

This is not to say that picking out invariants is always easy for an expert or that experts don't sometimes make mistakes. And experts can pick out different invariants over time because experts continue to learn and because domains of expertise change as discoveries are made and theories change. The point is that, at a given time, experts are usually faster and more accurate than novices in identifying critical invariants in their domain. When they're not, you should ask for your money back.

Chicken-sexing provides a fascinating example of experts' ability to pick out invariant properties. Deciding whether a baby chick is male or female can be very important. In some locales, there may be regulations against owning roosters within city limits. Also, one

may want to limit the number of roosters one has because they sometimes fight. Or a farmer may want only hens and the eggs they produce.
Therefore, farmers often want to know the sex of newly hatched chicks
so they can keep the females, and "sacrifice" the males. To do so, they
hire a chicken-sexer, an expert in distinguishing male and female
chicks. This is not an easy task. It is an art developed in Japan. The
chick has an external opening called the *cloaca*, which serves diges-
tive, urinary, and reproductive purposes. This opening is closely examined for a degenerate penis, which is found in all males but also 15%
of females. The developed skill of a professional chicken-sexer is in
determining the sex of this 15%. It requires effort and many hours of
training and practice. Novices are not much better than chance at
determining a chick's sex.[3] But experts get faster and faster. The best
sexers in the world are able to sex about 800 chicks an hour with 99%
accuracy. They have so developed their ability to distinguish the male
from female pattern that they can do it instantly. In other words, they
have so trained themselves to pick out what's invariant about chicks
of each sex that they can make a decision based on that invariance
immediately.

The search for invariants is not limited to experts. It is something that we all do and can be observed at the lowest levels of
perception. Perception involves discovering the cues that consistently signal things of interest to distinguish them from noise. This
is why the tau variable is so useful. It refers to an invariant relation
between moving agents and the obstacles they could encounter and
so provides all the information that an organism needs to negotiate
its environment without bumping into things. A variety of variables
of this type have been identified by psychologists interested in how
we use information in the environment to control our behavior.

The father of this approach to the psychology of perception was
James J. Gibson.[4] He referred to these aspects of the environment
that we attend to and that control our behavior as "affordances."
Gibson believed that the world has invariant properties and relations that provide the necessary information to afford organisms the
opportunity to fulfill their perceptual goals. Gibson talked about
perception being "direct." Rather than conceiving of organisms as
processors of information who use sensory mechanisms to grab a
variety of evidence that is then processed to extract what is relevant
(recall the High Church view of cognition from chapter 1), Gibson
believed that organisms are built to respond directly to relevant
invariants in the perceptual stream. He believed that organisms can
be compared to radios. Radios don't compute; rather, they are tuned

to transmissions in the environment. Radio signals are out there ready to be received. For this analogy to work, you must believe that adequate information is already in the environment to allow people to accomplish their goals, that this information is invariant, and that people are somehow already tuned to pick up this and only this information.

This book does not endorse Gibson's approach as a general theory of how the mind works. For one reason, adequate information for achieving goals is not always in the environment but often must be constructed on the basis of memory and inference (imagine trying to fly a modern jet airplane without memory and inferential procedures!). But this book will endorse the idea that people search for invariants relevant to satisfying their goals and that those invariants are used to guide thought and action.

The focus on invariants can be observed beyond the perceptual system. In general, prediction requires identifying the variables whose behavior is constant over time so that their future behavior can be derived from their present values. Predicting the weather requires focusing on wind direction, pressure gradients, and so on because these are consistently related to changes in the weather. Explanation, like prediction, involves assimilating an observation or phenomenon to a process or representation that applies generally, that emanates from or instantiates relations that are regular. Explaining someone's behavior involves appealing to personality traits of that person that persist over time or to forces in the person's situation that would cause most people to behave that way. Beyond prediction and explanation, control requires knowing the systematic relations between actions and their outcomes, so the right action can be chosen at the right time. A good politician will know who is motivated by greed and who is motivated by larger principles in order to discern how to solicit each one's vote when it is needed. In all these cases, the secret is to identify and use invariance, the constant, regular, systematic relations that hold between the objects, events, and symbols that concern cognition.

In the Domain of Events, Causal Relations Are the Fundamental Invariants

Where should we look for invariance? It seems to be hiding. All around us, we see change. Patterns of light and sound come and go constantly as we move about, as the sun shifts, as someone speaks. People change over lifetimes, species over evolutionary time. The sun has even set on the British empire by some accounts. Everything that has a physical realization is transient. So those things that are physically realized, objects and events, do not wear invariance on their sleeve.

But it must be there. We wouldn't be as certain as we are that (say) money buys goods, gravity holds things to the ground, war will occur again somewhere, or that we'll take our next breath if we couldn't rely on some things not changing. In none of these cases does our certainty derive from direct observation by our senses. It's not the world itself that doesn't change; everything physical changes. It's the generating process that produces the world that doesn't change. For example, the process that produces trade doesn't change. People have desires and needs and the intelligence and social structure to realize a means to satisfy some of those desires, such that mutual benefit through trade is common. This process is causal; it involves causal mechanisms that turn supply and demand into trade. In the case of gravity, too, the invariant is the causal mechanism that produces gravity. It takes mass and distance from the center of a body and produces a force as an effect. It is constant and it is pervasive, though physicists debate whether it holds only in this universe or whether it holds in every possible universe. Either way, it is a good process to bet on if you are a mere mortal. It is as reliable an invariant as the laws of mathematics, though only the former is obviously causal.

So relations of cause and effect are a good place to look for invariance. The mechanisms that govern the world are the embodiment of much that doesn't change. They don't embody all invariants: mathematical relations are invariant without necessarily being causal. But they embody a good part. The physical world, the biological world, and the social world all are generated by mechanisms governed by causal principles.

The invariants picked out by the experts mentioned earlier all concern the operations of mechanisms. The electrician cares about how things are connected because the causal pathways that govern electricity are determined by electrical connections. Similarly for plumbing. The fall of a pipe matters because the mechanism that controls drainage involves gravity operating within the walls of a pipe. A psychologist focuses on human and not material relationships because our emotional health is always a function of our relationships to other people and related only weakly and indirectly to our material possessions. In later chapters we'll see that prediction does not always require appeal to causal mechanisms because sometimes the best guess about what the future holds is simply what happened in the past. But sometimes it does, especially when there is no historical record to appeal to. And we'll see that explanation and control depend crucially on causal understanding.

That causal relations are invariant should come as no surprise. After all, much of science is devoted to discovering and representing invariant causal structure (e.g., force changes acceleration, demand increases price, structure determines function, life requires energy, power breeds corruption). The causal principles that govern mechanisms are so useful because they apply so widely. They apply across time (yesterday, today, tomorrow), and they apply across large numbers of objects. Every physical body in the universe is subject to inertia, and every living organism consumes energy, now and always.

In sum, people are exquisitely sensitive to the invariance of causal relations, the relations that govern how things work. Notice it is not the working mechanisms themselves that are invariant but the principles that govern them. A car engine is a causal mechanism designed to be reliable and in that sense invariant, but—as we all know—that is a pipedream. Shadows are cast by objects that block a light source like the sun, but the precise form of the shadow-casting mechanism may change continuously as the earth rotates and clouds shift. The invariant is not the form that the mechanism takes but rather the principles that govern its operation. The drive shaft of a car is not invariant, but the principle relating torque to force is. And the sun-cloud mechanism that produces shadows is changing all the time, but the principles that govern how light and objects produce shadows are constant. Causal principles that govern how events affect other events are the carriers of information, and it is those principles, not the mechanisms that they govern, that persist across time and space. They are the most reliable bases for judgment and action we have.

One might argue, along with philosophers like Bertrand Russell,[5] that invariant laws aren't causal at all but rather mathematical. Metaphysically, this may indeed be correct. Perhaps the world is nothing but a flow of energy. Perhaps there is no will, no agents, no intentions, no interventions, just the transformation of energy following certain eternal mathematical rules. Perhaps there is no root cause of anything, and perhaps there is no final effect either. Perhaps everything we misconstrue as cause and effect is just energy flow directed by mathematical relations that have determined the course of history and will determine our destiny in a long chain of events linked by the structure of energy in time and space.

Maybe. But this book isn't about metaphysics. It's about representation. It's about how people represent the world and how we should represent the world to do the best job of guiding action. The central idea of the book is that the invariant that guides human reasoning and learning about events is causal structure. Causal relations hold across space, time, and individuals; therefore, the logic of causality is the best guide to prediction, explanation, and action. And not only is it the best guide around; it is the guide that people use. People are designed to learn and to reason with causal models.

3

What Is a Cause?

Causes and Effects Are Events

In everyday language, causes and effects assume various roles. We say drugs cause addiction, sparks cause fire, and guns cause death (or at least bullets do). In each case, an object (drugs, sparks, guns) is the cause of a state (addiction, death) or an event (fire). Physical and emotional states can cause other states, as fear causes loathing, hunger causes suffering, or satisfaction causes tranquility. Events can cause other events, as one war causes another, or a strong wind causes a tree to fall.

It's harder to think of cases when we say a physical object causes another physical object. Parents cause their children, in a sense, and factories cause their products, but these statements don't sound quite right. The reason such cases are hard to think of is that we conceive of objects in a static way, as if they are fixed over an extended period of time, yet causal relations are enacted over time.

A causal relation suggests a mechanism unfolding over time that uses the cause (and possibly other things) to produce the effect (and possibly other things). So the notion of cause involves change over time, whether the time interval is short (as a light source causes a shadow), long (as the big bang causes the universe to expand), or intermediate (as the earth's rotation causes the day to turn into night). One general temporal constraint on causation is that effects cannot precede their causes.

Although cause suggests mechanism, it's a mistake to try to define cause in terms of mechanism because that generally leads back to where we started. What's a mechanism? A dictionary might respond that a mechanism is a process by which something is done or comes into being. But this seems just an oblique way of saying that a mechanism is something that turns causes into effects, and that's exactly where we started. I have yet to see a definition of mechanism that doesn't at least implicitly use the notion of cause. The fact that we can't define "cause" and "mechanism" without reference to one another suggests that they're closely connected. I'll talk about mechanisms as any kind of process that takes causes and produces effects.

So causal relations relate entities that exist in and therefore are bounded in time. I will refer to such entities as *events* or *classes of events*, because the word "event" suggests the transient character of causes and effects. On closer inspection, all the examples I noted have this character. For example, drugs don't cause addiction per se; rather, the class of event "drug consumption" causes the psychological and physiological events associated with addiction. Guns themselves don't cause death; the event of a gun being shot can cause the event that a living thing dies. Sometimes we talk in a non-temporally bounded way as if abstract properties can be causes and effects (increases in pressure cause increases in temperature; love causes beauty). But even here, the actual causes and effects as they manifest themselves in the world are physical entities that obtain for periods of time.

This is what distinguishes causal relations from definitions. A definition identifies a word or phrase with a set of conditions in the world. If all the conditions are met, then the word or phrase applies (i.e., the conditions are *sufficient*). Likewise, if the word or phrase applies, then the conditions are met (the conditions are *necessary*). If an object is geometric and has three sides, then it is a triangle. And, if it is a triangle, then it is geometric and has three sides. Causal relations don't associate linguistic entities with conditions. They associate events with other events.[1]

Experiments Versus Observations

The first thing an experimental psychologist learns is to distinguish an experiment from a correlational study (actually, this is the second thing they learn; the first is that theory without data is like cake without flour: all sugar, no substance). A correlational study involves mere observation, what goes with what, when, and where (no why involved). Two attributes or variables are correlated if a value on one tends to be associated with a value on the other. Hat size is correlated with shoe size, the time on my watch is correlated with the time on your watch (assuming it's not broken), temperature is correlated with pressure. But the mantra of experimental psychology is that correlation is not causation. The fact that these things are correlated does not tell us *why* they are correlated. It does not tell us what generating mechanisms produced these correlations. To find out, we have to run an experiment.

Francis Bacon (1561–1626) was one of the earliest spokesmen for the advantages of the experimental method, when performed correctly: "For the subtlety of experiments is far greater than that of the sense itself, even when assisted by exquisite instruments—such experiments, I mean, as are skillfully and artificially devised for the express purpose of determining the point in question." Bacon thought an experiment was akin to torturing nature for its secrets: "For like as a man's disposition is never well known or proved till he be crossed, nor Proteus ever changed shapes till he was straitened and held fast, so nature exhibits herself more clearly under the trials and vexations of art than when left to herself."[2]

An experiment requires manipulation. Some variable, some potential cause (often called an independent variable), is chosen along with another variable, a potential effect (often called a dependent variable). The cause is then manipulated by setting it to two or more values and the effect is measured. If the value of the effect differs for different values of the cause, then we can infer that the cause has some influence on the effect; a causal relation exists. To illustrate, say you want to know if punishing children makes them more obedient. Then you need to vary punishment, the independent variable, by punishing some children more and other children less and measure their level of obedience, the dependent variable. If the children punished more are more obedient than the children punished less, and if the difference is big enough, you can conclude that punishment increases obedience. And if the children punished less are more obedient, then you have some explaining to do.

Much of the art of experimental methodology involves satisfying two requirements. First, the cause must be manipulated so that only the target cause is manipulated and not other potential causes accidentally. When manipulating punishment, you have to be careful not to also manipulate how much warmth you show the child. Second, the methodology must be sufficiently powerful to allow a reasonable assessment whether a difference in the value of the dependent variable is real or just the reflection of random variability.

I'll say more later about what experiments allow us to learn that correlational studies don't. For now, the important point is that conclusions are drawn from experiments through comparison; the value of an effect must be compared in two different worlds: the world in which the cause is at one value and one in which the cause is at a different value, because a causal statement is a claim about two (or more) worlds simultaneously.

Causal Relations Imply Certain Counterfactuals

To say that A caused B seems to mean something like the following: A and B both occurred, but if event A had not occurred (and B had no other sufficient cause), B would not have occurred either. The critical point is that a causal relation doesn't merely imply that events happened together but that there's some generating mechanism that produces an event of one type when engaged by an event of another type. So in some other world in which the mechanism had not been engaged by the cause, the effect would not have resulted. This is what distinguishes a causal relation from a mere correlation. A correlation between two event types means that they move together; when one happens, the other tends to happen, too. A causal relation has the further requirement of *counterfactual* dependence.[3]

A counterfactual is a statement that concerns another possible world.[4] "If only" statements are good examples of counterfactuals ("If only I had a million dollars." "If only my true love wasn't so tall." "If only I hadn't eaten so much last night."). All of these open thought or discussion about some other world, different from this one. Some counterfactuals are introduced by "almost" to bring into focus possible outcomes that didn't actually occur: "The Giants almost lost yesterday." "My lottery number almost came up." "I almost won the Nobel prize (unfortunately, my discovery was 150 years too late)." Counterfactuals actually appear in a huge variety of linguistic forms ("He could do it if he wanted to," "I would have been happy if I hadn't taken that job"), sometimes with no special markers ("It's the things you don't say that you regret the most.") Some counterfactuals aren't necessarily about other possible worlds but could be about this one ("She might have gone to the opera, but I think she went to the nightclub").

A causal relation assumes a counterfactual, one that is related to *the effect would not have occurred if the cause had not*. This is a counterfactual because in fact the cause did occur and so did the effect (or, at least, they may well have). But what makes the relation causal is that the cause is responsible for the effect in that (again) if it hadn't occurred, the effect would not have either. Correlations make no such counterfactual claim. Shoe size and hat size are correlated, but that doesn't mean that if my feet swell, my head will swell too. Correlations are just about what goes together in the actual world. They're not about how things would be if the world were different.

For the same reason, counterfactual dependence also distinguishes a causal relation from an "association," a favorite term of psychologists to talk about how events elicit thoughts and behaviors. An association between two events is normally assumed to be formed by an organism who perceives that the events are correlated.

In sum, causal relations are more than descriptions of the way things are, the state of the world. They are processes that generate possibilities, whether those possibilities exist—whether they are actual—or counterfactual. Causal relations tell you how you get there from here, whether you're actually going there or not. As generative processes, they differ fundamentally from correlations, for a correlation is merely a description of what's been observed. So the first (or second) law of experimental psychology holds: correlation is not causation.

The great Scottish philosopher David Hume taught that causation cannot even be inferred from correlation.[5] On logical grounds, no number of observations permits a causal inference. No matter how many times A and B occur together, mere co-occurrence cannot reveal whether A causes B, or B causes A, or something else causes both. But one of the million dollar questions today (actually, research funding agencies have spent well over a million dollars on it) is whether Hume was right. Some recent theories of causality specify how causal inferences can be drawn from correlational data in certain cases. I'll touch on that question later. It's worth mentioning, though, that Hume also taught that people make causal inferences in everyday life anyway, despite their lack of justification in doing so. This kind of unjustified causal attribution is all around us. When a new administration enters government and the price of gas rises, there's a strong tendency to blame the new administration. In this kind of case, very different causal attributions may have just as much support: the forces that led to a rise in gas prices may also have created the conditions for the new administration to be elected.

Enabling, Disabling, Directly Responsible: Everything's a Cause

So far I have pointed out that a causal relation implies a counterfactual. This isn't really saying much because people are not necessarily aware of the implied counterfactual; they may not know about it at any level. If you admit to chopping down the cherry tree, that doesn't necessarily mean that you're thinking, consciously or unconsciously, that the cherry tree could still be alive. Moreover, the relation between a cause and a counterfactual isn't simple, for it could depend on a host of other events.

Let's focus on a specific event to note how else it might have been and how all the other events responsible for that event (the *parent set* of that event) together determine how it might have been. Take your birth, for example. The events that together caused your birth include some actions by your mother, some actions by your father, the presence of food and oxygen in your mother's environment after conception, a favorable gestation, a safe place for birth, and so on:

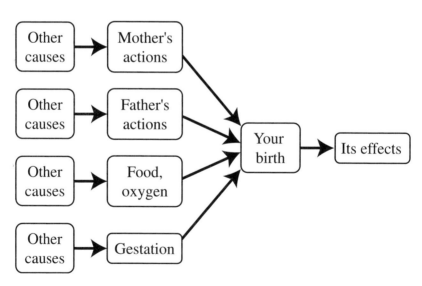

Figure 3.1

In an important sense, your mother's and father's actions are the "true" causes—they are at least the responsible people—while food, oxygen, and gestation are just "enablers" because they make the critical event (your birth) possible or set the stage for it. You can also imagine "disablers" that prevent an event, like a chemical exposure that causes a miscarriage. But such distinctions can become fine legal points. Is birth control a disabler or a true cause (of not giving birth)? What's clear and what follows without any legal or moral analysis is that birth would not have happened without *all* the precursors. The event might well have been different (counterfactually) if any of those parental events had been different. Who knows how you would have turned out if gestation had been different or if your mother had enjoyed a different diet? Therefore, for simplicity, we'll use the word "cause" in a general way, to refer to all precursors, all variables that would have led to a different effect had they been different. The notion of enabling and disabling conditions is useful, and I'll use it at various points. But at the most basic level, where we just want to know about the mechanisms that make events happen, it is very useful to divide the world up simply into causes and effects.

Causes don't always act in concert to produce events. Sometimes an event has alternative causes, each itself sufficient for the effect. Death can be caused by trauma, uncontrolled growth, infection, and so on. In rare cases, more than one can conspire to cause death together. The arrow-drawings or graphs like figure 3.1 that I'll use in this book don't mark the difference between cases where causes act together (conjunctively) or separately (disjunctively) to produce an effect. But later I'll make this distinction by representing the way causes produce effects as simple mathematical equations (what are known in the trade as structural equations).

Problems, Problems

To see some of the problems in defining cause, consider the following story.[6] Betty throws a rock at a bottle. Charlie throws a rock at the same bottle. Both of them have excellent aim and can break the bottle almost every time. Betty's rock gets to the bottle first and breaks it. Charlie's rock would have broken it, but it got there too late. Did Betty's rock cause the bottle to break? Of course. Did Charlie's? Of course not. Yet, under the counterfactual test, if Betty hadn't thrown her rock, the bottle still would have broken, just like the bottle would have broken even if Charlie hadn't thrown his rock. In terms of the events, Betty's and Charlie's situations are the same. Both threw rocks and a bottle broke. And counterfactually they are the same. Yet they're different: Betty caused the bottle to break;

Charlie didn't. What's the difference? Somehow it seems important that Betty's rock touched the bottle, whereas Charlie's didn't. We can spell out a detailed causal chain for Betty, not for Charlie.

If we asked a different question, who's more to blame for the bottle breaking, then the difference between Betty and Charlie seems smaller. They'd both better run if the owner of the bottle shows up.

A variant of this story concerns a sheik whose wife wants to kill him because she just found out about his mistress. The mistress wants to kill him anyway to steal his money. The sheik's going on a long journey through the desert, so the wife puts poison in his water sack. Just before he leaves, the mistress puts a small hole in the water sack so that his water drips slowly out and he dies of thirst in the desert. The wife then reports the mistress, who gets thrown in jail for murder. There's no evidence against the wife. But is she guilty?

These problems disturb philosophers because they undermine the very definition of a causal relation. I have defined A caused B in terms of counterfactuals; I said that A and B occurred and if A hadn't occurred, B wouldn't have occurred either. In our story the mistress connives to let the sheik die of thirst and he does die of thirst. She would seem to be the cause of his death. And the wife tries to kill him with poison but fails. So she doesn't seem to be the cause of his death (she may be guilty of attempted murder, but her failure would presumably block a verdict of guilty of murder).

Yet both women are in the same position with regard to the definition. Both acted; both had the desired effect achieved. The sheik is dead. However, and this is the critical point, *both would have achieved the desired effect even if they had not acted.* The counterfactual part of my definition of cause was that the effect would not occur in the absence of the cause. But in the story, the effect would occur (the sheik would be dead) if the wife had not acted (because the mistress would have killed him). So according to this definition, the wife is not the cause of death. Similarly, the sheik would be dead if the mistress had not acted (because the wife would have killed him). So my definition suggests that the mistress is not the killer either. The counterfactual definition suggests that neither is guilty, that neither is the cause of death because neither's action changed what would have happened anyway. There must be something wrong with the definition.

Any definition of cause must be more elaborate to account for this sort of complication (and others). The definition that I gave earlier actually was slightly more elaborate. It said that the counterfactual part matters only if event B were to have no other sufficient causes at the moment. But both women do have another sufficient cause of death. If the mistress fails, the wife will kill him, and if the wife fails, the mistress will kill him. If we were to rule out these alternative sufficient causes, if we ignored the wife when considering the mistress and ignored the mistress when considering the wife, then their respective actions indeed would be responsible for the effect. If we ignored the wife's poison, then the mistress's hole would be the difference between life (the counterfactual world) and death (the actual world), and vice versa for the wife. So this second definition that rules out alternative causes posits that both are, in fact, the causes of death.

We just can't get it right; both definitions fail to tell us that the mistress is the cause and the wife isn't. What's wrong with this definition of cause? At one level, it fails to be sensitive to the particular fine-grained causal pathway that takes us from action to effect. We can point to a chain of true causal links that take us from the mistress's action to the sheik's death (the hole in the canteen, the slow emptying of its contents on the desert floor, the sheik's look of surprise and dismay as he lifts the canteen to his lips, his gradual weakening from dehydration...). We can do no such thing for the wife because the sheik didn't die of poison. But in the end this doesn't solve the problem because of the critical words "causal pathway" in the description of the chain. I'm trying to define *causation,* but it seems like cheating to do so by appealing to a *causal* pathway. That's like the left hand paying a debt to the right hand. Maybe it's possible to describe this pathway without using the notion of cause by appealing to specific laws. Physical laws govern how water drips out of a canteen, for instance, and if we can describe the whole chain in terms of such well-known laws with independent motivation, we might be able to define cause without referring to cause.

Another possibility is to make the definition more sophisticated. This is what the legal philosopher J. L. Mackie did.[7] I'll present his idea briefly to offer a taste of it even though it's going to be a bit of a tangent. To really understand it, I recommend reading the original. Mackie pointed out that what we call a cause is actually a part of a larger entity. Whenever an effect is caused, a large number of true conditions in the world are responsible for it. If a rock breaks a bottle, it's because (1) the rock was heavy enough (but not so heavy that it couldn't be thrown); (2) the rock was moving at sufficient speed; (3) the bottle had sufficiently weak bonds holding it together; and so forth. Altogether, these conditions are sufficient for the effect, and anything we call a cause is part of such sufficient

conditions, indeed a necessary part because we wouldn't call it a
cause if the effect would have happened even if the condition referred to wasn't there. Of course, the set of conditions sufficient for
the effect aren't together necessary, because there may well be some
other set of sufficient conditions that would lead to the same effect.
So the condition at issue is a cause if it is Insufficient itself for the
effect, but it is a Necessary part of an Unnecessary but Sufficient set
of conditions. That's a mouthful both linguistically and conceptually. So Mackie called it INUS for short. A condition is a cause if it is
an INUS condition. This reduces the linguistic problem, but it still
leaves a conceptual mouthful.

To see how INUS solves our problem, think about the wife's
poisoned water and the mistress's hole in the canteen. The hole in
the canteen is one (I) of the critical elements (N) in one (U) of the
long set of conditions that must have obtained for the sheik to die
(S). So it was a cause of death. The poisoned water, in contrast, is
not a critical element of a sufficient set of conditions because the
set of conditions that include drinking poisoned water did not actually kill the sheik. It would have to include conditions like "the
sheik drank the poisoned water," but it can't because such conditions didn't actually obtain. It's critical of INUS conditions that
they refer to conditions that are actually true of the world. But
when an event didn't actually lead to an effect, then something has
to be not true of the world and the INUS condition won't be met.

The discussion in this section has been using the word "cause"
in a different sense from the rest of this book. As I'll discuss at
length in the next chapter, the rest of this book will use "cause" to
mean anything that can be represented by an arrow in a causal
graph. To foreshadow, both the wife's poisoning and the mistress's
puncture can be represented as arrows in a causal graph:

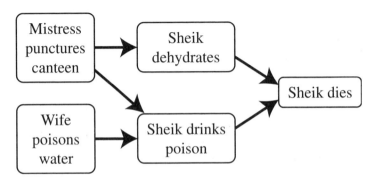

Figure 3.2

In that sense, all of these events (that may or may not occur) are causes. In this section, I have been discussing which event in a causal graph is the *actual* cause. Both the wife's and mistress's actions may be causes in the sense of being relevant in the graph, yet only the mistress's action (I think we agree) is the *actual* cause of the sheik's death.

The graph actually offers a simple explanation. There's a link from the mistress's puncture to the sheik drinking poison because the puncture *prevented* the sheik from drinking the poison (due to the puncture, there was nothing for him to drink). The puncture blocked the chain of events from the wife's poison to the sheik's death from coming to pass. There's no such preventive link from the wife's poisoning to the chain of events from the mistress's puncture to the sheik's death. So the reason that the mistress is at fault is because her action was not prevented from having its intended effect; the wife's action was prevented from having its effect.

Several philosophers have suggested that actual causes can be read off a causal graph using this kind of logic.[8] Very roughly, an event is an actual cause of another event if both of the following are true:

1. Both events actually occurred.
2. If the first event had not occurred (counterfactually), then the second event wouldn't have either, even when all events not on the causal path from the first to the second are assumed to have occurred (as they actually did).

If we assume that the canteen was punctured and the sheik dehydrated, then no change to the amount of poison would prevent the sheik from dying. Hence, the wife's poisoning is not a cause. In contrast, if we assume that the wife poisoned the water but the sheik didn't drink the poison—what actually happened—then the mistress's puncture is the difference between life and death. So the mistress is guilty.

This kind of analysis doesn't provide a definition of cause that's independent of cause. After all, it depends on chains of arrows, and arrows are nothing but causes. What it does do though is offer an idea about how people go about determining what the actual cause of an event is from a bunch of causal knowledge.

Could It Be Otherwise?

A frequent problem with scientific theories, especially theories of how the mind works, is that they are too powerful. A theory that can explain everything, both what is true and what is false, in the end explains nothing at all. A parody of such a theory would be one that attributes thought to a little person in the head (a homunculus). If the explanation of how I think is that another person is thinking for me, then we haven't gotten anywhere at all. This would just be the tip of an explanatory circle in which X is explained by Y, which is in turn explained by X.

But we have to be careful, because theories that have this essential character often come dressed in other clothes, so it's hard to identify their circularity. Consider a simple theory that attributes all learning and memory to associations. Learning consists in the construction of associations between things in the world or between actions and things in the world. (A theory like this was once made very popular by B. F. Skinner.) Notice just how powerful a theory it is. Whatever you tell me you've learned, I can describe the associations that you've constructed. If you've learned a language, then I can wave my hands about the associations between objects and words, and the associations between parts of speech like nouns and verbs that you must have acquired. But, of course, I could describe an infinite number of associations that you haven't learned, too. I never learned that "outside" means where clouds are, even though, where I come from, one usually sees clouds when one goes outside. So the real question is what's the difference between the things you have learned and the things you haven't. Simply listing them after we already know they exist, even in the form of a list of associations, doesn't help. Because the theory can explain everything, it explains nothing. Of course, sophisticated theorists are aware of this problem, so good associationist theories do say more. Generally, they describe the process of learning in some detail.

The problem of circularity is pervasive when people try to explain mental processes as the result of evolution. I, for one, am a great believer in an updated version of Charles Darwin's process of natural selection. One of the beauties of natural selection is that it is so simple and yet so powerful that it provides an explanation for the origin of all living things from the primordial soup to current, complex biological organisms. It is therefore tempting to use it to explain the most impressive biological entity around, the human mind. After all, presumably the mind did originate during a process of evolution. It may also have been the side effect of the evolution of other functions (my favorite is the idea that the mind developed alongside the brain, which evolved as a large-scale cooling system for the rest of the body). Nevertheless, there has got to be some evolutionary story about how the human mind came to have its current form. The problem is that there is also an evolutionary story for how the mind did *not* turn out. The theory of evolution, because of its elegant simplicity, is powerful enough to allow the construction of a plausible story for any possible mind that didn't happen to evolve. The trick is merely to find some adaptive function that such a mind served and then dramatize why that function was so important in the era of greatest change to the species. Evolutionary theory is a powerful source of stories, so good evolutionists are careful when they go about storytelling, always making sure that they have enough facts to warrant a theory and that their theories stay close to those facts.

Does the notion of cause suffer from the same problem? Is it so powerful a concept that it can explain everything, even what is not observed?

Not All Invariance Is Causal

Not only is the notion of cause not general enough to explain all possible properties of the mind, even those that don't exist; it is not even so general that it can explain all properties that *do* exist. Some of the invariance that people are sensitive to is not causal at all.

People pay attention to part-whole relations, for example. We are experts in recognizing how nose, mouth, eyes, cheeks, compose a whole face or how abstract shapes compose an abstract pattern, like a plaid. We immediately perceive how the parts of a view—the people, objects, the background—relate to make up a scene. The human capacity to recognize and create patterns out of parts is masterly (pigeons are pretty good at it, too, it turns out). People are also sensitive to relations among classes (e.g., that a chicken is a fowl and a hammer a tool). Syntactic structures in language are not causal (although, as we'll see in chapter 11, they, too, encode some causal properties).

So people appreciate and use a variety of relations that are not causal. Many of these relations can be described using other kinds of logic, like set theory. Set theory is a well-developed branch of mathematics useful for talking about various kinds of relations. For instance, a part-whole relation is reminiscent of the relation between a subset and a set; a subset is a part of a set. A nose is a part of a face; the features that make up a nose are a subset of the features that make up a face. Set theory is also useful for thinking about relations among classes or categories. For example, according to the current American tax code, the class of trucks includes the subclass sports-utility vehicle (SUV). In other words, the set of SUVs is a subset of trucks (according to the U.S. Internal Revenue Service anyway). But not all set-subset relations are the same. Part-whole relations—known as *partonomies*—differ from subclass-class relations—*taxonomies*—in that a subclass is a member of the class, whereas a part is not a member of the whole (an SUV is a truck, but a nose is not a face). Also, a subclass inherits all the properties of the class, whereas a part does not inherit the properties of the whole (everything that is true of a truck is by definition true of an SUV, but plenty of things are true of faces—like their ability to display emotions—that are not true of noses).

Sets support all kinds of logical relations. If A is a member of B, and B is a member of C, then A is a member of C. If A is true and B is true, then "A and B" is true. And people are highly sensitive to much of this structure. But set theory is severely limited in what it can easily represent. As we'll see, it is unable to represent the logic of causal intervention.

Probability theory also captures invariance. But much of the invariance it describes results from the operation of causal mechanisms. The reason that the probability of rolling double-six with two fair dice is 1/36 has to do with counting the possible causal outcomes of rolling the dice separately. The reason that the weather forecaster predicts rain with probability .7 generally has to do with a causal model that predicts future weather outcomes by extrapolating from current conditions. The reason that the conditional probability is high that the ground is wet, given that it has rained, is that the former is a causal effect of the latter. So the invariance of probabilities is really just causal invariance in disguise.

Admittedly, not all probability relations have a causal basis. Quantum effects in particle physics are probabilistic, and philosophers argue about whether or not they have a causal basis. But such effects are notoriously hard for people to think about, so they don't provide much of a challenge to a causal model of thought. Also, some probabilities reflect degree-of-belief, not causal mechanisms. My subjective probability that the ancient Sabines inhabited a powerful city state reflects confidence, not causality. But even my confidence is generated by causal mechanisms, like the ease of recalling paintings and stories of Sabines and causal explanations about why Sabines might seem familiar.

In general then, causal relations are not the only kind of invariance useful for representing the world. There are various kinds of mathematical representations, as well as logical and probabilistic representations. But noncausal forms of invariance are less useful than causality for describing relations among events because they don't naturally describe the processes that generate those events and because, therefore, they fail to support key forms of counterfactual inference as directly as causal models do. In short, only causal models represent the invariance that tells us what the effects of our and others' actions would be. As a result, people seem to be particularly adept at representing and reasoning with causal structure.

4

Causal Models

Hopefully you now agree that, at least according to human perception, the world is full of causal systems composed of autonomous mechanisms that generate events as effects of other events. In this chapter, I will try to make this idea more precise and therefore more clear by making it more formal. I will introduce the causal model framework as an abstract language for *representing* causal systems. First, I will discuss it as a language for talking about causal systems. Later, I'll talk about what parts of it might have some psychological reality. These are not the same, of course. You might have a great system on your computer for bookkeeping, but the very reason you have it on your computer is because you don't have it built into your mind. Similarly, there are excellent systems for representing causal relations that might or might not describe how people think about causality. So let's start with a really good system for representing causality before we talk about how people do it.

The causal model framework was first spelled out in detail in a book published in 1993 by Spirtes, Glymour, and Scheines. The framework is based on a mathematical theory for representing probability called Bayesian networks. Many computer scientists, statisticians, and philosophers have contributed to its development, but I will rely to a large extent on the very complete treatment offered by Judea Pearl in *Causality*, published in 2000. The framework is a type of graphical probabilistic model. It's probabilistic in that it allows uncertainty or ignorance about whether an event will occur. It allows us to reason about events when we are unsure about what has happened, what will or would happen, and even about how events lead to one another. All we have to know is how likely events are and how likely they are to be caused by one another. In particular, causes don't always have to produce their effects; they only have to produce them sometimes.

The framework doesn't insist on probabilistic relations, however; if a cause always produces an effect, that is, if the cause and effect are related deterministically, that's all right, too. The framework is graphical in that a graph composed of nodes and links (like the graph of your birth in the previous chapter) represents the causal structure of a system, with nodes corresponding to events or variables in the causal system, and directed links (arrows) between nodes corresponding to causal relations.

The Three Parts of a Causal Model

In this kind of scheme, three entities are involved in the representation: the causal system in the world (i.e., the system being represented), the probability distribution that describes how likely events are to happen and how likely they are to occur with other events—how certain we can be about each event and combination of events—and a graph that depicts the causal relations in the system (see fig. 4.1).

In this picture, a link from one entity to another means the second *represents* the first. The probability distribution and graph both represent the world, and the graph also represents the probability distribution. Representation is a key concept here. In this context, a set of symbols represents a set of elements if the symbols are related to one another in the same way that the elements being represented are related to one another. A highway map is a representation of a region if the distances between places on the map are proportional to distances between corresponding places in the region. A caricature of Abraham Lincoln is a representation of Lincoln because the parts of the caricature's face are related to one another in the same way that the parts of Lincoln's own face were related (though the caricature's relations might be exaggerated). A representation has to be simpler than the thing being represented because it abstracts from the thing being represented; it mirrors some aspect of it. A representation can't mirror all aspects; if it did, it wouldn't be a representation, it would be the thing itself.[1]

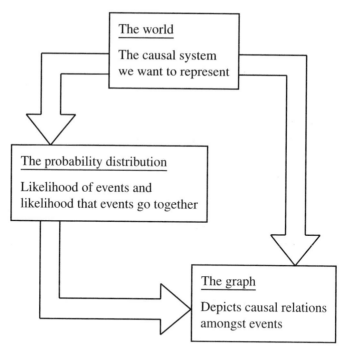

Figure 4.1

Probability distributions are representations of the world because they capture certain relations in the world. Namely, they
specify how much confidence we can have that an event will occur
or that an event will occur if we know that another one has.[2] They
are also simpler than the world because they don't specify everything about it. They don't specify, for example, how good an event
is, only how much confidence we can have in its occurrence.
Graphs are representations of probability distributions because they
specify the causal relations among events that are implicit in the
probabilities. In other words, they depict the causal relations responsible for the probabilistic ones. They are simpler than probability
distributions because they don't show every probability; rather, they
show only the structure of the causal mechanism that generates the
probability distribution.

Let's illustrate with fire, a causal system in the world that we're
all familiar with that relates sparks, oxygen, an energy source to
feed it, as well as other things, as shown in figure 4.2.

The probability distribution consists of a set of marginal probabilities and conditional probabilities. A marginal probability is the
raw probability of an event like the probability of fire, written P(fire),

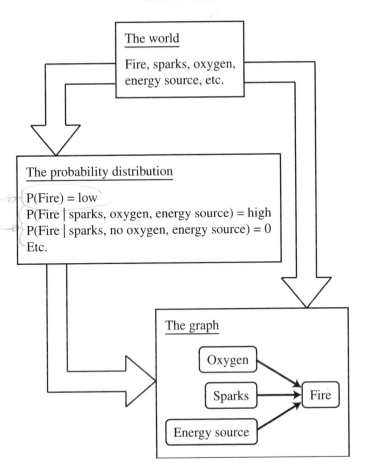

Figure 4.2

or the probability of sparks, P(sparks). A conditional probability is the probability of an event once you know the value of one or more other events. If you know there are sparks and oxygen and an energy source around, then you might ask what the probability of fire is, given this knowledge, conventionally written as P(fire | sparks, oxygen, energy source), where the symbol | means "given." Some people believe that all probabilities are conditional probabilities because all probabilities are assigned based on some knowledge.

Independence

The graph represents the causal relations in the system, and it constrains what the probability distribution can look like. For instance, if there's no path between two events in the graph, then this should be reflected in the probability distribution. For instance, music is unrelated to fire, so if the presence of music were included in the causal system, it would be represented as a disconnected node in the graph:

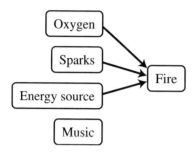

Figure 4.3

The probability distribution would reflect this by making sure that

$$P(\text{fire}) = P(\text{fire} \mid \text{music}) = P(\text{fire} \mid \text{no music}).$$

In English, the marginal probability of fire is the same as the conditional probability of fire given music and also the same as the conditional probability of fire given no music. This relation between fire and music is called independence because the probability of fire is the same whether music is playing or not.

In sum, a causal model representation has three aspects: the world being represented, an algebraic representation of it in terms of probabilities, and a graphical representation of the causes that generate the probabilities. One of the most important aspects of the world captured in both the probabilistic and graphical representations is independence, when events have nothing to do with each other. Every time we can say events are independent, we have said something important because it simplifies the graph by removing links and makes it easier to do calculations with probabilities. The most significant qualitative information in a causal model is that two events are independent, because independence lets us simplify, and simplification while maintaining veridicality (accuracy) is the key to an effective representation.

Structural Equations

It is easiest to think about the graph and the probabilities as parts of a single representation. You can do so by associating each node of a causal model with a set of probabilities or conditional probabilities.

Each node is the joint effect of all links pointing into it. Fire is the joint effect of sparks, oxygen, an energy source, and so on. So the effect (fire) is fully described by stating the probability of fire under all possible combinations of its causes:

P(Fire | sparks, oxygen, energy source) = high
P(Fire | sparks, oxygen, no energy source) = 0
P(Fire | sparks, no oxygen, energy source) = 0
P(Fire | sparks, no oxygen, no energy source) = 0
P(Fire | no sparks, oxygen, energy source) = very low
P(Fire | no sparks, oxygen, no energy source) = 0
P(Fire | no sparks, no oxygen, energy source) = 0
P(Fire | no sparks, no oxygen, no energy source) = 0

To keep the variables simple, I'll assume that each takes on one of only two possible values—present or absent—even though in reality each variable is essentially continuous (the fire could be any size and there could be various quantities of sparks or of oxygen, etc.). Even with this simplification, $2^3 = 8$ conditional probabilities (all possible combinations of the presence or absence of sparks, oxygen, and energy source) would be required to describe this one little mechanism producing fire. To describe the causal system fully, we'd also need to know the marginal probabilities of sparks, of oxygen, and of an energy source. So a lot of numbers are necessary ($8 + 3 = 11$). But these 11 numbers would be a complete representation of this common causal system.

The goal of structural equation modeling is to make the representation smaller and more elegant by specifying how the causes combine to produce the effect. Causes can come in many forms. Some are direct causes, others enabling or disabling conditions. Multiple causes might produce an effect jointly or individually. They might add up or multiply to produce the effect.

Structural equation modeling expresses the precise nature of the functional relation representing the mechanism determining each effect using a different representational scheme than probabilities and graphs, but one that carries the same information (technically speaking, an isomorphic representation). Each effect is associated with a mathematical function expressing exactly how it is produced by its causes. For example, if a spark, oxygen, and a source of energy are required to produce fire, the following equation could represent a causal mechanism:

Fire = f(spark, oxygen, energy source)

where f means conjunction—that all causes are required. The way I've written this equation ignores the fact that the function is actually probabilistic. A more proper equation would include an additional variable that would be called error or noise. It would represent the contribution of sources of randomness that make the relation probabilistic.

This equation is a more compact and simple way of writing what is expressed by the long list of conditional probabilities shown. Instead of describing the mechanism as a list of the probabilities of the effect for each possible combination of causes, it describes the mechanism more directly by expressing how the causes are combined to produce the effect. Causal graphs are good for expressing a complex system of causal relations; structural equations are good for expressing the specific function relating a set of causes to their effect.

What Does It Mean to Say Causal Relations Are Probabilistic?

A causal relation is probabilistic or is affected by random factors if the combination of known causes isn't *perfectly* predictive of the effect. Some combination of causes might usually produce the effect but not always; conversely, the effect might usually be absent in the presence of certain causes yet occur sometimes nevertheless.

Sources of randomness can sometimes be reduced to other causal mechanisms that we happen to be ignoring. The wind is an important factor in whether a fire occurs, but it makes sense to consider the causal mechanism of a spark mixing with oxygen and fuel to understand the physics of fires and to understand the key controllable ingredients. So we might ignore the wind and treat it as a random factor. And there could be other random factors, such as how dry the environment is and the ambient temperature. Sometimes our fire doesn't start even though all the critical elements are there, but instead of causally explaining why not, we just attribute it to one of the various random factors. These factors are random only in the sense that we're ignoring them by bundling their effects into a single variable that we call random that makes the functional relation between causes and effects not perfectly predictable but rather probabilistic.

Some theorists believe that some types of probability are not due to what we ignore, but rather are due to intrinsic unpredictability in certain causal mechanisms. For instance, some physicists consider some phenomena of quantum physics to be intrinsically probabilistic. We won't have to worry too much about this possibility, though. For the kinds of medium-scale causal systems that people tend to think about in everyday life, randomness is produced by what we ignore, not by the fundamental nature of events.

Causal Structure Produces a Probabilistic World: Screening Off

One of the central ideas of the causal modeling framework is that stable probabilistic relations between the observed variables of a system are generated by an underlying causal structure. In other words, the world we see around us with all its uncertainty can be attributed to the operation of a big, complicated network of causal mechanisms. On a smaller scale, particular kinds of causal structure will lead to particular patterns of probability in the form of particular patterns of dependence and independence.

Let's see how direct causal relations depicted by arrows in a graph correspond to relations of dependence and independence. In the simplest case, if we ignore the direction of arrows in a causal graph and see that there's no route from one variable to another, if the two variables are disconnected, those two variables should be unrelated, or probabilistically independent. In contrast, if a causal arrow points from one variable to another, they should be related, or dependent. In the case of a *causal chain*:

Figure 4.4

A and C should be dependent because A is an indirect cause of C. Imagine that A is lightning, B is fire, and C is heat.

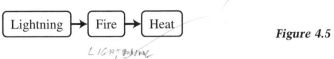

Figure 4.5

On this model, wind and heat are dependent because you're more likely to have heat if you have lightning than if you don't have lightning. Changes in A should produce changes in C. But if we hold B fixed, A and C should be independent because the effect of A on C is mediated by B. In more static terms, A tells us nothing about C when we already know the value of B. In particular, if we know there's a fire of a certain size, then we learn nothing about the presence of heat by learning whether there's lightning. Similarly, if we know there isn't a fire, knowing about lightning doesn't tell us

The Markov condition

anything additional about heat. A and C may be dependent, but they are *conditionally independent given B*. This is one example of what mathematicians call the Markov condition, or what psychologists call the "screening-off property" of causal graphs. B screens off A from C by virtue of mediating A's causal effect on C.

Screening off also arises with *causal forks*:

Figure 4.6

In this case, B is a common cause of both A and C. For example, let A be damage and B and C again be fire and heat, respectively. Because B causes both, A and C are again dependent (they tend to occur when B does and not to occur when B doesn't). So the relation between A and C is again mediated by B. As a result, if we fix B, A and C are no longer related; they are independent conditional on B. If we already know there's fire, or if we know there's no fire, learning there's been damage tells us nothing new about the presence of heat. So the conditions for screening off are also met with a fork: A and C are dependent but independent conditional on B. B screens A off from C.

The third basic kind of relation among three variables is known as a collider or *inverted fork*:

Figure 4.7

In this case, B is a common effect of both A and C. Let A be lightning and C a smoldering cigarette and B again is fire. In this structure, A and C are independent if the value of B is unknown because they have no common causes and they don't cause each other. The probability of lightning doesn't change if there's a smoldering cigarette on the ground. But if B is known, then they become conditionally dependent. If we know there's a fire, then the probability of lightning decreases if we learn there was a smoldering cigarette because the cigarette explains the fire. The fire provides less evidence for lightning because the fire is already explained. This is called explaining away and will be discussed in chapter 6 in the context of discounting.

Equivalent Causal Models

I just claimed that observed probabilities are generated by causal models and that therefore knowledge of causal structure allows us to make inferences about dependence and independence. Conversely, given the observation of certain dependencies and conditional dependencies in the world, one can infer something about the underlying causal structure. Say you measured A and B at various points in time and you noticed they changed together: when one is high, the other tends to be high; when one is low the other tends to be low (in statistical terms, they are correlated). In other words, they are dependent. This could occur for many reasons. A could be the cause of B,

Figure 4.8

or B could be the cause of A,

Figure 4.9

or A could be an indirect cause of B,

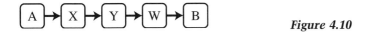

Figure 4.10

or both could be caused by some other variable V,

Figure 4.11

Indeed, you could produce many other causal models explicating why A and B are dependent. Some of these possibilities could be tested by examining other dependencies. For instance, if A turned out to be independent of X, then the chain in which A is an indirect cause of B could be ruled out.

Let's consider the possibilities with only three variables, A, B, and C. If you know that A and B are dependent and also that A and C are dependent but independent given all possible values of B, then A and C must be causally related and B must screen off A from C. Only three causal models that relate A, B, and C to one another are possible to express these relations.[3] The first two are chains and the third is a fork.

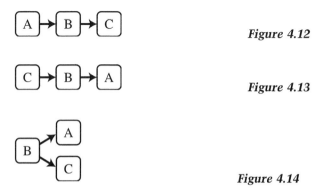

Figure 4.12

Figure 4.13

Figure 4.14

These are called Markov-equivalent (this is different from the Markov condition!) because they cannot be distinguished using relations of independence/dependence or indeed any kind of mere probabilistic information alone. Some other kind of information is required, like the temporal order in which the three events occur or the effect of an intervention, as I'll discuss in the next chapter.

Inferring Causal Structure Is a Matter of Faith

Making inferences from dependencies in the world to causal structure requires two assumptions concerning the relation between a causal graph and the probabilistic patterns of data it generates. Recall that the parent of a variable X is the set of all variables that feed into X, all its causes considered together. The first assumption says that a variable's parents screen it off from the parents' parents (its grandparents and other ancestors, if you like). This assumption, known as the *causal Markov condition*, suggests that the direct causes of a variable—its parents—render it probabilistically independent of any other variables except its effects. This a very useful assumption, because in practice it means that we can determine the value of a variable by examining the value of the variable's parents along with the values of its effects, if we happen to know them. We don't have to go back through chains of indirect causes. This condition will hold so long as a causal graph explicitly represents any variable that is a cause of two or more variables in the graph.

The second assumption, the *stability assumption* (sometimes called *faithfulness*), stipulates that any probabilistic independencies in the data should arise solely because of causal structure and not because of mere chance. Imagine we flip two coins A and B. We win $10 if they come up the same (both heads or both tails), and we lose $10 if they come up differently. A and B are obviously independent events: P(A is heads|B is heads) = P(A is heads) = .5. Paradoxically, winning is also apparently independent of both A and B: P(WIN|A is heads) = P(WIN|A is tails) = P(WIN|B is heads) = P(WIN|B is tails) = P(WIN) = .5. That is, whether A comes up heads or tails, the probability of winning is .5; similarly for B. Moreover, the overall probability of winning is also .5. The likelihood of winning apparently has nothing to do with the outcome of flipping either A or B, yet, causally speaking, winning is completely determined by the outcomes of A and B:

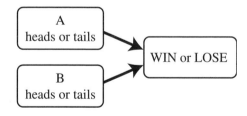

Figure 4.15

Notice, though, that the apparent independence disappears if the probability of A and B is anything other than .5. Imagine that A and B are biased; they have bits of heavy gum stuck onto one end such that they come up heads three out of four times. A and B are still independent: P(A is heads|B is heads) = P(A is heads|B is tails) = P(A is heads) = 3/4. But winning is no longer apparently independent. You win if both come up heads, which happens with probability $3/4 \times 3/4 = 9/16$, or if both come up tails, which happens with probability 1/

$4 \times 1/4 = 1/16$. So the probability of winning is the sum of these possibilities: $P(\text{WIN}) = 9/16 + 1/16 = 10/16 = 5/8$. But if you know that A is heads, then you win only if B comes up heads, which happens with probability 3/4. So the probability of winning given A is heads is $P(\text{WIN}|A \text{ is heads}) = 3/4$, which is not the same as $P(\text{WIN})$. Now WIN is dependent on A (and B by similar reasoning) as it should be.

To conclude, the apparent independence between winning and the outcomes of the coins was limited to the very special case where $P(A \text{ is heads}) = P(B \text{ is heads}) = .5$. It's really just a coincidence of values, not a true relation of independence. The stability assumption is that *stable* independencies arise from the structure of a causal model, not from mere coincidence. The result of flipping coin A is independent of the result of flipping coin B in this sense because the coins have no causal influence on one another. Two variables are expected to be truly unrelated or independent in the absence of certain kinds of causal paths between them. In contrast, *unstable* independencies arise from some coincidental set of values of the conditional probabilities in the model. Situations can arise when two variables satisfy the definition of probabilistic independence yet are causally related, as in the example just described of winning if, and only if, two fair coins both take on the same value. Such situations are unstable in the sense that the apparent independence disappears as soon as one of the relevant probabilities changes. In the example, winning was no longer independent of the coins once we imagined that the coins were no longer fair but instead had a probability of heads different from .5.

By assuming that unusual coincidences of value of this kind don't arise very often in the world and that they therefore can be ignored, we can use independence to help us decide on the true causal structure among variables. We make this stability assumption all the time in real life. For instance, we generally assume that if we see one person, then we should assume that there is only one person present, not that there's another person behind the first in exactly the position that would obscure the second person. The probability of two (or three or four...) people when all you see is one is so low that it should be neglected. The causal model analog is that we should assume that the independencies we observe arise from actual causal mechanisms and not from highly unlikely coincidences. The assumption derives from the desire to pick out stable mechanisms rather than transitory events.

In sum, patterns of probabilistic relations, dependence and independence, imply certain causal structures; from relations of independence we can infer something about the underlying causal system. To do so, we have to make two reasonable assumptions about how the world works. By assuming screening off, that indirect causes (ancestors) have no effect when parents' values are fixed, and stability, that independence is not coincidental but arises only in the absence of causal relatedness, we can infer a lot about causal structure by observing the world and in some cases can identify it uniquely. Sometimes we cannot identify a unique causal structure, but we can still limit the set of possible causal structures to a Markov-equivalent set: those causal structures consistent with our observations.

The Technical Advantage: How to Use a Graph to Simplify Probabilities

The reason that statisticians and people interested in artificial intelligence care about all the fine details of graphs and probability distributions is that graphs can be used to simplify calculations; sometimes they help so much that they make calculations possible that would otherwise be just too hard. By representing what variables are independent of one another, graphs tell us what we can ignore. Often, much can be ignored.

I'll now try to explain how graphs help, although I won't do so with mathematical precision, and I won't even try to justify the claims (I'll leave that to more technical expositions). The following discussion is a little technical, as technical as this book will get, and you can skip it without losing the thrust of the rest of the book. But it's worth looking at, if only briefly, as it's the mathematical heart and soul of graphical probability models. It's why theorists bother with this kind of method.

Consider a small causal system composed of eight binary variables (A, B, C, D, E, F, G, H: each takes two values, say **on** and **off**). A complete probabilistic description of this system is called a joint probability distribution and is written as follows:

P(A, B, C, D, E, F, G, H).

To fully specify the joint probability distribution requires that we state the probability of all possible combinations of the variables' values):

P(A = on, B = on, C = on, D = on, E = on, F = on, G = on, H = on) = p_1,
P(A = off, B = on, C = on, D = on, E = on, F = on, G = on, H = on) = p_2,
P(A = on, B = off, C = on, D = on, E = on, F = on, G = on, H = on) = p_3,
etc.

If we spelled out all individual probabilities, we'd end with $2^8 - 1 = 255$ p values. (2^8 because there are 8 variables with 2 values each. We subtract 1 because the sum of all the ps must equal 1.0; the probability that the system is in one of the 256 states is 1.0. Therefore, we can figure out the last p by subtracting all the other ps from 1.0.) Each p is a parameter of the system so we see that a full description requires 255 parameters.

But if we know something about the structure of the causal graph that relates the variables, we can use that knowledge to reduce the number of parameters needed to describe the system. Imagine that the variables are related in the following way:

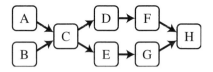

Figure 4.16

This graph shows a lot of independence relations among these variables: A is independent of B, and A and D are conditionally independent given C, along with many other independence relations. These independence relations can be taken advantage of to rule out many of the joint probability distribution's parameters. The trick is to read the joint probability off the graph starting from the root nodes (the initial causes) and progressing through the causal graph by following links. The fact that variables' values depend only on their parents and not on their parents' parents allows a simple technique for writing the joint probability distribution in a simple form. In this case, it turns out that

$$P(A, B, C, D, E, F, G, H)$$
$$= P(A) \cdot P(B) \cdot P(C|A,B) \cdot P(D|C) \cdot P(E|C) \cdot P(F|D) \cdot P(G|E) \cdot P(H|F,G).$$

Notice that we obtain the new form by conditioning each variable on its parents. This equation may look scary, but in fact it is a lot simpler than specifying the probabilities of each state individually. To describe it fully requires knowing $P(A)$, a single number or parameter, $P(B)$, another parameter, as well as the conditional probabilities. They require more parameters. $P(C|A,B)$ requires four:

$$P(C = on \mid A = on, B = on)$$
$$P(C = on \mid A = on, B = off)$$
$$P(C = on \mid A = off, B = on)$$
$$P(C = on \mid A = off, B = off)$$

Again, we don't need the probability that C is off because that can be obtained by subtracting the probability that C is on from 1.0. P(D|C), P(E|C), P(F|D), and P(G|E) require two parameters each, and finally P(H|F,G) requires four. So, all told, we need 18 parameters once we take into account the structure displayed by the causal graph. That's an immense savings over the 255 required without using that structure. In many cases, the 255 parameters would be unobtainable. For instance, if we have to run an experiment to obtain each one, we'd have to run 255 experiments and we may not have time or money to do so. But if we only need 18 parameters, obtaining them may well be possible.

Some real-life causal systems have hundreds or thousands of variables. Think of all the relevant variables in a political system or in a modern airplane. The space shuttle has about a quarter of a million operational components. The more variables a system has, the more potential savings there are from parameter reduction if we have a causal graph that we can trust.

5

Observation Versus Action

The discussion so far has focused on observation, what our causal graphs suggest that we can expect to see in the world and what our observations of the world allow us to infer about causal structure. And probability talk seems a good way to talk about what we observe and what we should expect to observe. But there's more to causality than that. Causality doesn't just tell us what to expect as passive observers, but what to expect when we take action, when we act as agents and intervene on the world. Causality concerns the effects of the actions we take. It also concerns the effects that actions that we don't actually take would have were we to take them. Causality at the most fundamental level concerns action, and I have not yet provided a means to represent action in the formalism. I will now introduce such a means, but first a note about representing observation.

Seeing: The Representation of Observation

The structure of a causal graph, in combination with the probability distribution across its nodes, determines what inferences we can make on the basis of new information. When this information takes the form of an observation, when we see or hear or learn about in some other way the value of a variable in our model, then we must change the probabilities of all other variables, given this new information. This process of changing probabilities to reflect new information is called updating, and a simple theorem of probability theory can be used to do it.

The theorem was first discussed by the Reverend Thomas Bayes in 1763 in a letter entitled "An Essay Towards Solving a Problem in the Doctrine of Chances"; therefore, it is generally referred to as Bayes' rule. One school of thought among philosophers is that probabilities are essentially representations of belief, that probabilities reflect nothing more than people's degree of certainty in a statement. Even an assertion that would seem to have a strong objective basis, like the belief that a randomly chosen die is fair—that the probability of each of its six faces coming up when rolled are the same and equal to exactly 1/6—can't be fully justified by analysis or by experience. It can't be proven by analyzing the die because, after all, the faces cannot all be *exactly* the same size and the distribution of mass within the die will ever so slightly tilt the die in favor of one face or another. You could roll the die many times in order to see empirically if the faces have equal probability. But to answer the question with any confidence would require a huge number of rolls, so many that the die would have changed shape by the time you had collected enough observations. The change in shape may be very slight, but even a tiny change could affect the probability of the die coming up 1 or 6 or something else.

You could argue that you don't know which face is more or less likely, and therefore they should all be given equal probability. I think this is a good argument, but it's a claim about what you don't know, not about the way the world really is, and in that sense it's saying that probabilities are grounded in knowledge, in a subjective mental state. For this reason, philosophers who believe that probabilities are representations of belief are sometimes called subjectivists because they claim that probabilities are grounded in subjective states of belief. Sometimes these philosophers are called Bayesian because Bayes' rule turns out to be extremely important on their view.

One argument that has been raised against subjectivism is that if probabilities are grounded in the beliefs of a judge, then it would seem that the judge can make the probabilities anything they want them to be. If a subjectivist wants the probability that a particular horse will win the race to be high, then what is stopping him or her from simply believing and asserting that the probability is high?

The answer is that even a subjectivist's probability judgments have to make sense. They have to *cohere* with all their other judgments of probability, and they have to correspond with what is known about events in the world. This is how Bayes' rule helps; it prescribes how to take facts in the world into account in order to revise beliefs in light of new evidence. That is, it dictates how to change your probability judgments in the face of new information—how to update your beliefs or, in other words, to learn—while maintaining a coherent set of beliefs, beliefs that obey the laws of probability.

Other schools of thought about the foundations of probability also exist. The most prominent alternative to subjectivism is frequentism, which supposes, roughly speaking, that a probability reflects a long-run relative frequency of an event (the probability of a die landing on 6 reflects the proportion of times it would land on 6 if it were tossed an infinite number of times). But it's beyond the scope of this book to discuss the foundation of probability in any detail.[1] I'll just point out that Bayes' rule isn't specific to subjectivism. It's a rule about how probabilities relate that holds whatever your philosophy of probability.

Bayes' rule looks like this. Say you have some hypothesis about the world, perhaps that your friend Tatiana has a bacterial infection. Call it D (for *d*isease) and its antithesis, that Tatiana does not have a bacterial infection, $\sim$D ($\sim$ can be read as *not*). Assume you have some degree-of-belief that D is true, P(D) [P($\sim$D) is just $1-$P(D)]. P(D) is often called a prior probability of D because it represents your degree-of-belief before you come across new evidence about Tatiana. Say you do encounter new evidence relevant to D; for instance, it turns out that Tatiana has a peptic ulcer. Call this new datum S (for *s*ymptom). You also have some belief about the effects of D: peptic ulcers are a symptom of bacterial infections. But you know that peptic ulcers can arise for other reasons, $\sim$D. For example, they might also arise as a result of consuming too much aspirin.

Now you need to revise your belief in D in light of S. But how should you go about it? You want to know P(D|S): the probability of the disease given the symptom or, in this case, the probability that Tatiana has a bacterial infection, given that she has a peptic ulcer. Bayes' rule tells us what it is:

$$P(D|S) = \frac{P(S|D)P(D)}{P(S)}.$$

P(D|S) is called a posterior probability because it is the probability of the disease *after* taking into account the evidence provided by the symptom. Bayes' rule is very easy to prove using the mathematics of probability. But conceptually it's not that simple. Why should our belief in D given S be related to the probability of S given D and the prior probabilities of D and S in just this way? Instead of trying to answer this question directly, we'll look at it in a way that makes more intuitive sense.

Let's think about what we want to know (how likely it is that Tatiana has a bacterial infection) in a form that doesn't require that we calculate P(S) directly. Instead of calculating the probability of the hypothesis given the data, we can figure out another quantity: P(D|S) divided by P(~D|S), the odds of the hypothesis after taking the data into account, called the *posterior odds*. This tells us how much more or less likely the hypothesis is than its complement, P(~D|S). Knowing the odds that our hypothesis is true rather than false is as useful to us as knowing the probability that our hypothesis is true.

I showed Bayes' rule for P(D|S). But I could have just as easily written it, in a completely parallel form, for the complementary hypothesis that Tatiana does *not* have a bacterial infection:

$$P(\sim D|S) = \frac{P(S|\sim D)P(\sim D)}{P(S)}$$

To calculate the odds, P(D|S)/P(~D|S), all we have to do is divide the first equation by the second (this is the only bit of algebra I'll do in this book!). This gets rid of P(S) by dividing it out:

$$\frac{P(D|S)}{P(\sim D|S)} = \frac{P(S|D)}{P(S|\sim D)}\frac{P(D)}{P(\sim D)}$$

That's enough mathematics. You can think about this equation as having three parts: the posterior odds, P(D|S)/P(~D|S); what I'll call the *likelihood ratio*, P(S|D)/P(S|~D); and the *prior odds*, P(D)/P(~D). The prior odds is just the ratio of our prior probabilities, the odds that the hypothesis is true before taking the evidence into account. The equation shows that the three parts are related in a very reasonable way:

$$posterior\ odds = likelihood\ ratio \times prior\ odds.$$

Our belief after incorporating the new evidence S (the posterior odds) is equal to whatever our belief was before (the prior odds) times the likelihood ratio.

The likelihood ratio tells us how strong the evidence S is for or against D. Specifically, it tells us how well S distinguishes D from

~D. Tatiana has some probability of having a peptic ulcer by virtue of D, a bacterial infection. But she also has some probability of having a peptic ulcer by virtue of ~D, having consumed too much aspirin or for some other reason. The higher the former probability and the lower the second, the higher the likelihood ratio will be. The likelihood ratio is the odds that the new fact (Tatiana has a peptic ulcer) would arise if the belief we're concerned about (Tatiana has a bacterial infection) is true relative to it being false. Learning about the peptic ulcer will help us diagnose whether Tatiana has a bacterial infection only if peptic ulcers are either much more probable given bacterial infections than given other reasons, or if they are much less probable. If their probabilities are roughly the same, then the likelihood ratio will be close to 1 and learning about the peptic ulcer won't tell us much.

The likelihood ratio requires knowing $P(S|D)$ and $P(S|\sim D)$. These are quantities we can usually obtain. If we have some belief about the way the world is (knowledge about what produces peptic ulcers), then we generally know what to expect when various diseases occur (the probability that a bacterial infection will result in a peptic ulcer and that other conditions will lead to a peptic ulcer). The likelihood ratio is really important and valuable because it is so simple yet it tells us so much. It tells us how well the data—new facts—discriminate one belief from another, and when you're deciding what to believe from observations, that's what determines the value of information.

Let's summarize how we learn about Tatiana from observation. We start with some belief that Tatiana has a bacterial infection, denoted by the prior odds. We then learn that she has a peptic ulcer. So we multiply the prior odds by the ratio of the probability that she has a peptic given that she has a bacterial infection with the probability that she has a peptic ulcer for some other reason (because she's consumed too much aspirin, say). If this ratio is greater than one (we believe that peptic ulcers are more often caused by bacterial infections than aspirin), we end up with a posterior odds greater than the prior; we increase our belief that she has a bacterial infection. But if the ratio is less than one because we think peptic ulcers are more likely to be a result of aspirin, we lower our posterior odds; we decrease our belief in bacterial infection.

This logic based on Bayes' rule is natural and may be familiar to you. We start with a degree-of-belief in the way the world is; we look at the world; if the world is consistent with our beliefs, then we increase our degree-of-belief. If it's inconsistent, we decrease it.

In fact, if we do this long enough, if we have enough opportunity to let the world push our probabilities around, then we would all end up with the same probabilities by updating our beliefs this way. Bayes' rule is guaranteed to lead to the same beliefs in the long run, no matter what prior beliefs you start with.

Notice how important symptoms are for determining disease according to this logic. Our beliefs tell us which diseases lead to which symptoms. But by learning about someone's symptoms (observables), we can make good guesses about the disease they have (an unobservable). This is the technical sense of *diagnostic*: effects (symptoms, in this case) help us figure out the causes (diseases, in this case) that must have been present through the kind of backwards inference exemplified by Bayes' rule.[2]

Action: The Representation of Intervention

Presumably the point of all this belief formation and updating is to know how the world works, what the causal mechanisms are that guide it. In chapter 3, we learned that the way to find out about causal structure is not through mere observation but through experiment and what distinguishes the two is that experimentation requires action; it requires intervening somewhere in the system. Imagine that instead of observing values, we bring them about ourselves through our action. What if we get rid of Tatiana's peptic ulcer by giving her Grandma's special formula? All we know about Grandma's special formula is that it goes directly to the ulcer, bypassing all normal causal pathways, and heals it every time (unfortunately, Grandma passed away taking her formula with her or we'd be rich). Before our intervention, our causal model of peptic ulcers looked something like this:

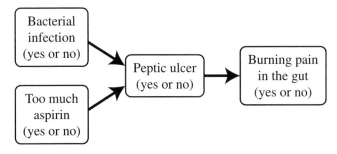

Figure 5.1

Our direct intervention with Grandma's special formula warrants a change in our belief that Tatiana has a peptic ulcer (i.e., we should now believe that she doesn't), but because we're the ones that got rid of her peptic ulcer, we had no effect on the normal causes of that ulcer. Tatiana is just as likely to have a bacterial infection or to have consumed too much aspirin as she was before we applied Grandma's formula. Therefore, we should not change our belief in the probability of those causes. We should not make a diagnostic inference from the absence of Tatiana's peptic ulcer to the presence of bacteria or her consumption of aspirin because those *have nothing to do with the absence of the peptic ulcer*. We should act as if the normal causes of peptic ulcer are independent of the ulcer because they no longer have an effect; we're the ones that got rid of the ulcer.

Graphically, the relevant causal model after intervention temporarily looks like this:

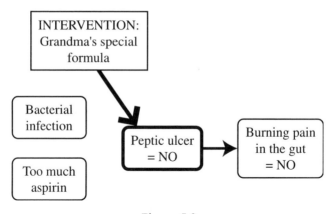

Figure 5.2

Our intervention on peptic ulcer had three effects. First, it set the value of peptic ulcer to NO because Tatiana no longer has one. Second, and less obviously, it changed our causal model by cutting peptic ulcer off from its normal causes so that the absence of the ulcer would not be treated as diagnostic of those causes. Third, because the intervention did not cut peptic ulcer off from its effects, only its causes, it also reduced Tatiana's burning pain in the gut. After all, if Grandma's magic formula gets rid of Tatiana's ulcer, it should also relieve the pain from the ulcer, whatever the cause of her ulcer. We can make this inference because the link from peptic ulcer to burning pain remains intact.

The general lesson is that the inferences that we can draw after *observing* a particular value of a variable are not the same as those that we are licensed to draw after *intervening* to set the variable to that same value ("no ulcer" in the example). Bayesian updating by itself fails to recognize this difference. We cannot use Bayes' rule to figure out the probability of a cause after intervening to set an effect because the links between cause and effect no longer exist; the intervened-on effect is not diagnostic of its causes.

The absence of peptic ulcer suggests nothing about the presence of a bacterial infection or about aspirin intake after intervention on the peptic ulcer. Of course, we don't need to use Bayes' rule because things are simpler with intervention. The probability of the cause is whatever it was before our intervention; no updating is necessary.

Acting and Thinking by Doing: *Graphical Surgery*

What's new and different about the causal modeling framework is that it gives us a way to represent intervention and distinguish it from observation. To do so, Pearl[3] introduced the *do* operator. To represent intervention on a variable X in a causal model by setting X to some value x, we *do*(X = x). Previously, we did the equivalent of

$$do(\text{peptic ulcer} = \text{NO}).$$

The *do* operation doesn't only set a variable to a value; it also modifies the causal graph by disconnecting X from its normal causes. Because an agent is acting to determine the value of X, the normal causes of X have no influence on it. The action overrides the causes of X, rendering them irrelevant. Otherwise, the graph remains the same. Pearl calls this a surgery. The graph is surgically altered by removing one specific connection and leaving others intact. The effects of the intervention are then computable through normal probability calculations on this "mutilated" graph.[4] In other words, the *do* operator is exactly what we need to take us from the first causal model to the second. As a result, it allows us to represent actual physical intervention (like applying Grandma's special formula). It also allows us to represent intervention in our minds, counterfactual intervention, by imagining what would happen *if* we did something (like apply Grandma's formula, which, if truth be told, doesn't actually exist). It gives us a way to represent another possible world that we might imagine or fantasize about or pretend to live in or use to make an argument (mothers love possible-worlds arguments: "If you were more considerate, then people would like you more". So do professors: "If you had done the analysis the way I did, then you wouldn't be stuck in this quagmire"). It even tells us how to represent that other possible world. Start with the causal model of the world you're in, choose the aspect of that world that you want to be different, *do* it by changing that aspect as specified by the counterfactual assumption (i.e., set its value to the value imagined), and then cut it off from its causes. You'll end up with a new causal model of the new world you're thinking about, but one that's very similar to the old world. In fact, as long as the variable we're intervening on is not a root node in the causal graph (a variable with no known causes), the new world will be a simplified version of the old world, one with fewer causal links. If it is a root node, we'll end up in a world with an identical causal structure.

The representation of an imagined (counterfactual) intervention is obtained in exactly the same way that the representation of an actual physical intervention is obtained. Hence, the two graphs of Tatiana's medical concerns before and after intervention with Grandma's special formula illustrate the inference process, even if we're only imagining what would happen if it were applied. The only real difference in reasoning about actual versus counterfactual intervention is that the graph after intervention represents the actual world in the case of actual intervention but another possible world in the case of counterfactual intervention. To reason counterfactually, you make an assumption. You might imagine that Tatiana has no peptic ulcer, *do*(peptic ulcer = NO); or that the moon were made of cheese, *do*(moon's composition = CHEESE); or that Tatiana loved me, *do*(Tatiana's love interest = STEVEN); and so on. Then trace through the implications of the assumption to see what its effects are (the moon would be covered with mice and people who love cheese, etc.). What you don't do is change the normal *causes* of the facet of the world whose value you're assuming, only its effects. You don't assume that the big bang led to a lot of cheese pervading the universe that coalesced into the moon. Such an assumption would be irrelevant. Instead, you consider the consequences of a cheesy moon.

Science fiction authors do this all the time. They make an assumption, often known to be false (there is life on Venus; everyone has access to a mind-altering wonder drug without any side effects), and draw out the implications of their assumption. To question the validity of the assumption would involve pointing out how the normal causes of that aspect of the world would never lead to the assumed state ("Venus is too hot to support life and it has no water anyway"), but that would be uncooperative and seems pedantic. We assert things all the time in order to capture their effects ("If only there was life on Venus, then I could find a friend"). Questioning whether the assumption is valid fails to address the issue. What matters is what that asserted world would be like, not whether it is possible.

In the simplest cases, the disconnection involved with the *do* operator separates a small chunk of a causal model from the rest of a larger model so that we can limit our stream of inferences to the smaller subset. The *do* operator has the effect of biting off a small part of our big model of the world and limiting our thinking to that part. Thus, we can use the *do* operator to think about a fictional world without changing our beliefs about the real world. Or we can use it to help us focus on some relatively small problem, like how to fix our car or what the results of an experiment should be, without worrying for the moment about the much bigger and more complicated world outside our current problem.

Computing With the Do *Operator*

Once we have the *do* operator, we can ask questions like what would be the probability of a bacterial infection if I eliminated the ulcer using Grandma's special formula? Using the *do* operator, this would be represented as

$$P(\text{Bacterial infection} \mid do(\text{peptic ulcer} = \text{NO})),$$

or what would be the probability of burning pain in the gut if I eliminated the peptic ulcer,

$$P(\text{burning pain in the gut} \mid do(\text{peptic ulcer} = \text{NO}))?$$

These are questions about *interventional* probabilities rather than *conditional* probabilities. The first interventional probability is equal to the prior probability of bacterial infection,

$$P(\text{Bacterial infection} \mid do(\text{peptic ulcer} = \text{NO})) = P(\text{Bacterial infection})$$

because peptic ulcer has been disconnected from bacterial infection and so provides no information about it. The second is identical to the corresponding conditional probability because the intervention has no effect on the relevant causal link:

$$P(\text{burning pain in the gut} \mid do(\text{peptic ulcer} = \text{NO}))$$
$$= P(\text{burning pain in the gut} \mid \text{peptic ulcer} = \text{NO}).$$

How do we calculate interventional probabilities in general? As we've just seen, we can read them off a fully specified causal model. In the example, if we know P(Bacterial infection) and we know the causal model as shown, then we know P(Bacterial infection| *do*(peptic ulcer = NO)). The trick is to reduce interventional probabilities to some combination of probabilities and conditional probabilities. We have to be careful if there are what Pearl calls "backdoor paths." This occurs when some other causal route links bacterial infection to peptic ulcer even after the links to the causes of peptic ulcer are removed, as would be the case if this were the operative causal model:

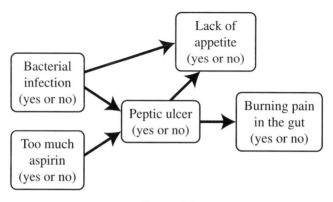

Figure 5.3

According to this model, peptic ulcers and bacterial infections are both causes of lack of appetite. So if you intervene to get rid of someone's peptic ulcer, you're likely to change their appetite. But a change in appetite can be informative about its causes, one of which is bacterial infection. So because of the backdoor path between bacterial infection and peptic ulcer that goes through appetite, intervening on peptic ulcer does not render it independent of bacterial infection. In such a case, extra precautions need to be taken to evaluate interventional probabilities in terms of conditional probabilities using the model. Calculations of interventional probabilities can get difficult, although there are software packages that can help.

Another way to evaluate an interventional probability is to run an experiment. If we collect a group of people and give them Grandma's special formula, then as long as Grandma's formula does not produce bacterial infection as a side effect, we can find out how many have bacterial infections, and that's our answer regardless of any backdoor paths.

The Value of Experiments: A Reprise

Now that I've spelled out how to represent observation and how to represent intervention, I can say more about observational studies, scientific studies that tell us only about whether variables are correlated or not and compare them more fully to experiments, which involve intervention. First, we see that the primary importance of observational studies is that they tell us whether variables are dependent or independent. And if we have enough data that we give sufficient credibility to, we can even tell if variables are conditionally independent or not. So there's a lot of information in correlational studies that measure the right variables. They can really narrow down the correct causal model. For any given three variables (e.g., intelligence, socioeconomic status, and amount of beer consumed per week), we can reduce the number of possible relations among them to three or four. For example, as we saw in the last chapter, if two of the variables are dependent, say, intelligence and socioeconomic status, but conditionally independent given the third variable, then either they are related by one of two chains

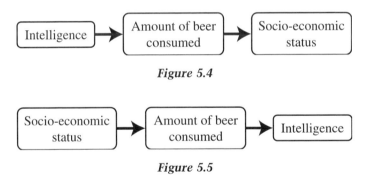

Figure 5.4

Figure 5.5

or by a fork

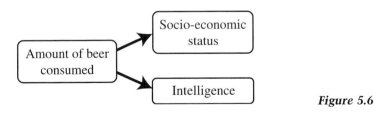

Figure 5.6

and we then must use other means to decide between these three possibilities. In some cases, common sense may be sufficient, but we can also, if necessary, run an experiment. If we intervene and vary the amount of beer consumed and see that we affect intelligence, that implies that the second or third model is possible; the first one is not. Of course, all of this assumes that there aren't other variables mediating between the ones shown that provide alternative explanations of the dependencies.

If we choose our variables wisely, then every correlation derives from a causal model of some sort. In general, a dependency between two random variables A and B could result from any of the following causal models.

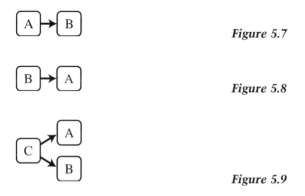

Figure 5.7

Figure 5.8

Figure 5.9

So we need a fair number of correlations, correlations conditional on other variables, and experiments to allow us to infer the right causal model given the large number of variables in most real causal systems. That's why learning causal systems can be hard. Indeed, some causal systems, like the solar system, required thousands of years of intense study before they were figured out, in part because nobody was able to run an experiment to vary the movement of the planets! But even when we can run experiments, causal systems can elude description. How the mind works, for example, is still a wide open question. Think of all the relevant variables. At the lowest level of description, everything that a mind can ponder is a cause of the mind's operation, and every thought and action that the mind can produce is an effect.

The Causal Modeling Framework and Levels of Causality

The conception of intervention that I've developed in this chapter draws on the idea that the directed links in a causal graph represent local, autonomous, and stable mechanisms. Intervening to set a variable to a fixed value disrupts those mechanisms that previously controlled that variable but leaves all other mechanisms intact. Further, it formalizes the intuitive notion that X causes Y (directly or indirectly) if some subset of interventions to change X *would* lead to a change in Y. It is this synergy of the concepts of causal link, mechanism, and intervention that gives the causal model framework its originality and power.

I have been talking as if the world is composed of one very large, very complicated set of causal mechanisms. But in fact the world is composed of many such sets because we can talk about causal systems in the world at different hierarchical levels.

A causal graph represents a causal system at a particular level of granularity. Causal systems afford multiple descriptions, though, at multiple levels of description. The human body can be described coarsely, in terms of its physiological systems (nervous system, cardiovascular, etc.) and how they interrelate, or, more finely, each physiological system could be decomposed into its parts. Clearly, this could be done at multiple levels of precision. The most specific level describes a particular causal event in terms of all of its contingent subevents, all relevant variables and their interactions and effects. One view is that a causal analysis at this level is deterministic because it describes every causal factor without ignoring anything (for the sake of discussion, we leave aside quantum indeterminism, as it probably has little to do with everyday causal models). Of course, descriptions this precise may not be possible, so such deterministic models may be merely ideals. As soon as variables are ignored, descriptions become more coarse. We almost always do ignore variables. If we ask whether smoking causes cancer, and certainly if we do so in a nonscientific context, we tend to ignore other contaminants in the environment, what people are eating, the shape of a person's lungs, all factors that could well contribute to cancer and to smoking's effect on cancer. This is when causality becomes probabilistic.

Causal analyses are hierarchical in another sense as well, in terms of their level of abstraction. A particular causal relation at its most specific level of description is a realized mechanism; at its most general it is a causal principle for generating mechanisms. For example, a particular guillotine is a specific causal mechanism. The mechanism depends on some abstract causal principles, one being that gravity causes acceleration. Note that general principles apply at every level of granularity, and, in this sense, these two kinds of hierarchy are independent. A plausible psychological hypothesis is that people store relatively few causal models, and certainly few at a detailed level of analysis. Instead, people may store general causal principles that allow them to construct causal models—and thus explanations for events—on the fly. As a result, people's causal models may usually be quite impoverished. Psychologist Frank Keil argues not only that they are but that people don't know just how impoverished they are![5]

II

EVIDENCE AND
APPLICATION

Part I introduced the theory of causal models. Part II
focuses on application. Each chapter investigates how
ideas about causality and causal modeling help to answer
various questions in cognitive science and examines the
evidence concerning the theoretical approach outlined in
part I. Each chapter looks at a selection of questions on a
different topic area in cognitive science.

6

Reasoning About Causation

The causal modeling framework suggests that causal considerations permeate how people reason. In this chapter, I discuss three kinds of reasoning that illustrate the central role of causality. The first part shows that causal considerations enter into how people think about some mathematical equations, that their thinking about equations reflects an underlying causal structure. The second part concerns social attribution, reasoning about why people do things. I show that people's explanations of behavior depend on the causal model that they believe governs that behavior.

The final part concerns reasoning about counterfactual events. In chapter 5, I discussed how counterfactual reasoning is a form of intervention. Thinking about a counterfactual world (like a world in which you have a million dollars) can be done by first imagining this world (the world in which you have only the amount of money that you actually have) and generating a causal model of it, and then intervening on that causal model by making a counterfactual assumption, for example by imagining something true that you know to be false (that you in fact have a million dollars). Here, I report evidence for this claim about how people reason counterfactually.

Each topic in this chapter requires progressively more of the causal model framework to explain how people reason. Together, they make a strong argument that reasoning with causal models is a natural, automatic, and efficient way for people to come to conclusions.[1]

Mathematical Reasoning About
Causal Systems

In chapter 2, I mentioned that Bertrand Russell, one of the great philosophers of this century, believed (or at least said) that there's no place for causality in true science: "The law of causality, I believe, like much that passes muster among philosophers, is a relic of a bygone age, surviving, like the monarchy, only because it is erroneously supposed to do no harm."[2] Although he seems to have changed his mind to some extent 35 years later,[3] the young Russell's view is instructive because it reveals an essential tension about the role of causation in science. One problem that has bothered scientists and philosophers of science over the years is that causation has often been associated with *determinism*, the idea that events follow necessarily from their antecedents without any room for probability or uncertainty. This concern isn't so relevant here because the causal model framework takes a fundamentally probabilistic view of causal processes. Beyond determinism, Russell believed that scientific theory should be expressed in terms of predictive, mathematical relations. A nice, elegant equation expresses so much so much more clearly than a complex causal story that often entails a variety of exceptions and boundary conditions that require specification.

I'm not going to argue with Russell about how science should be done, although I will make the observation that science is full of discussion of causality. The word "cause" may not appear in the titles of articles in hard science journals (they tend instead to be full of complex Latin jargon undecipherable to the uninitiated), but causality is at the heart of discussions in textbooks, seminars, and coffeehouses in both Cambridges (Massachusetts and England). You can see this by opening any popular science magazine. The central questions of physics, biochemistry, and neuroscience, as well as psychology and sociology and so on concern how mere mortals should conceive of their world in causal terms.

Speaking of mere mortals, many studies have shown that students use general knowledge about the way the world works, sometimes causal knowledge, to solve word problems in physics and mathematics.[4] Instead of thinking about problems in a purely abstract way, manipulating symbols until arriving at the correct answer, people solve problems guided by an understanding of the situation. If the situation is causal, then we use a causal model. Billiard players don't use equations to figure out the trajectories of their balls.

Players could do more calculations than they do. Billiard balls bounce off the rails of a pool table at the same angle they hit it; the incidence and reflection angles are the same. But people rarely think in terms of the "reflection law" per se. Instead, they make judgments based on intuitive models of billiard ball causality. This is most obvious when players use spin to help direct a ball. To plan the shot, players construct causal models in their minds that make predictions like "when the ball turns this way, then it will go this way and bounce off that way." People are known to impose a causal frame even when it distorts a representation. For example, people assert a unidirectional causal relation between variables that interact dynamically. The circuit between a battery and a light is often incorrectly understood as unidirectional, with energy flowing from the battery to the light.[5]

Here's another example. Say you're riding in an elevator and the cable breaks. There you are falling very fast to the ground in the elevator. Could you jump right before the elevator hits the ground and not be hurt? One way to solve this problem is by finding an equation that estimates your terminal velocity and another that estimates your momentum at impact from the terminal velocity you calculated, as well as your mass. Another way to solve the problem uses a causal model of falling. Imagine trying to jump while in a free-falling box at breakneck speed (how would you push off and what effect would your pushing off have on the elevator?). Reasoning from a causal model seems more natural than reasoning from a set of equations and is more likely to give mere mortals (nonphysicists anyway) the right answer. Don't bother trying to jump. Most nonexpert reasoners may even find the answer provided by causal reasoning more convincing than the mathematical answer, even though it's less precise. Deriving an answer in a way that uses our natural thought processes provides more certainty and comfort than a method that seems imposed by a textbook. When we use our own thought process, we don't have to rely on faith in an authority.

Solving physics and mathematics problems requires equations that must be constructed or retrieved from memory. One idea psychologists have had is that equations are embedded in organized bodies of general knowledge called schema.[6] When the schema is retrieved from memory, the desired equation is retrieved along with it. For certain kinds of problems this won't do; the equation may be completely novel and therefore has never been put in memory. For example, if all the teams in the National Football League (16 teams in each of 2 conferences) played every other team once, each team playing once per week, how long would football season be? In such a case, the equation must be constructed on the spot.

Equations are not mere collections of symbols; they are understood as expressing meaning themselves.[7] When you see

$$\mathbf{A} = \mathbf{l} \times \mathbf{w}$$

you probably think "area equals length times width," and you probably have a mental image of a rectangle with a length and a width that together combine to produce the area. The equation corresponds to a way of conceiving of a geometric relation. In this case, the relation is not causal, but the same conceptual modeling occurs in the causal domain. For example, we might write

$$\mathbf{p} = \mathbf{w}/\mathbf{a}$$

as a way of expressing

$$\text{pressure} = \text{weight}/\text{area}.$$

Doesn't this seem more natural than

$$\mathbf{w} = \mathbf{p} \times \mathbf{a}?$$

Mathematically, the forms are identical. Equations are symmetric in the sense that any variable can appear on either side of an equality, $X = YZ$ is identical to $Y = X/Z$. Algebra is all about how to permute the order of variables in equations without changing the relations that the equation expresses. But somehow the different forms aren't all the same for people. People don't treat equations in a purely algebraic sense; instead, equations have a conceptual function beyond their mathematical one; they provide a tool for thinking. Specifically, in the causal domain, equations are not understood symmetrically but rather in correspondence with the conceiver's causal model.[8] Algebraically, $\mathbf{p} = \mathbf{w}/\mathbf{a}$ and $\mathbf{w} = \mathbf{p} \times \mathbf{a}$ express exactly the same mathematical relation. But conceptually, the first equation is more intuitive because it corresponds more closely to a causal model. It's easy to think about weight being a cause of pressure in the sense that if you increase the weight of an object, that will cause it to exert more pressure. But it's hard to imagine how pressure could cause weight. Changing the pressure of an object won't change its weight in any obvious way. As a result, people are happier with pressure = weight/area than weight = pressure × area because, conceptually speaking, weight and area are causes of pressure, but pressure and area are not causes of weight.

Daniel Mochon and I have verified this claim in the laboratory.[9] Using a variety of different mathematical equations relating causally linked entities, we showed that people will reliably select a particular form of an equation over others as the causal version. It turns out that the form they select is the one that they consider most understandable. When asked to pick the version that they believe someone would find easiest to learn, the form that makes the most sense and would thus be easiest to teach a beginner, people had a strong preference to pick the same causal version. We know that the selected form corresponds to their causal model of how the variables in the equation influence one another because we asked people what their causal models were. Specifically, we showed the three variables of an equation (e.g., area, weight, pressure) and asked people for each one to "imagine that someone changed that variable" and then to circle the variables that they thought would change as a consequence. In most cases, they thought that the two variables they had treated as causes when picking out forms of an equation (e.g., weight and area) would not change but that the variable they had treated as an effect (e.g., pressure) would change. In causal model terms, the preferred model was:

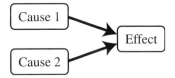

Figure 6.1

Finally, we showed that people have a strong preference for the form of an equation that matches their causal understanding when free to write any form they want. We gave them variables that were related causally in an obvious way but were not related by a known equation (e.g., growth rate, birth rate, death rate) and asked people to make up an equation relating them. They tended to isolate the effect (growth rate) on one side of the equal sign and put the causes (birth rate and death rate) together on the other side.

In sum, the form of an equation reflects the conceptual structure being represented. When the conceptual structure is causal, equations are understood and written down in a way that corresponds to a causal model. As Russell noted, science is replete with mathematical equations describing the laws of nature. Such equations are useful for several reasons. They make it easy to derive predictions and to calculate values. But despite the young Russell, they also provide a concise and exact representation of how variables relate conceptually while revealing the variables that are and are not relevant to a phenomenon. The conceptual relations might be geometrical, they might reflect mere numerosity, or they might be causal. Whatever they are, people seem to understand the equation in terms of its underlying structure. Equations don't have to be understood that way. After all, equations are merely collections of symbols that can be manipulated in some ways but not others. But people apparently don't normally understand them that way; instead, they understand them in terms of the structure of the world that they represent.

Social Attribution and Explanation Discounting

Social psychologists have studied people's causal analyses of human behavior for a long time. Consider a person's response that has two possible causal explanations. For example, the response might be Jim's belief that everyone's talking about him that could be caused either by Jim's paranoia, or by the fact that everyone is indeed talking about him. Here's a causal model to describe such a situation:

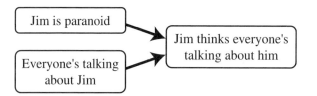

Figure 6.2

The fact that there's no direct link between the two causes in this causal model is equivalent to the assumption that knowing whether one of the causes is true or not tells us nothing directly about whether the other cause is true or not; the two causes are *marginally independent*; that is, whether Jim is paranoid or not doesn't depend on whether or not people are talking about him. Each of these causes is individually sufficient for the effect; Jim will think everyone's talking about him if they are in fact talking about him or if he's paranoid.

In a causal structure like this, if you know that the effect has occurred, and you have no other relevant information, then that raises the probability of both causes. Knowing that Jim thinks everyone's talking about him increases the probability (a little) both that he's paranoid and that everyone is in fact talking about him. The effect is diagnostic of its causes. However, if you know that the effect holds, the knowledge that one of the causes occurred (e.g., Jim is diagnosed as paranoid) makes it less likely that the other cause is the reason for the effect (it's less likely that everyone's in fact talking about him). In probability jargon, the causes are not *conditionally* independent; they are dependent conditional on the effect. In other words, even though

$$P(\text{cause 2} \mid \text{cause 1}) = P(\text{cause 2}),$$

knowing about cause 1 tells you nothing about the probability of cause 2 so that the two causes are marginally independent; it's also true that

$$P(\text{cause 2} \mid \text{cause 1, effect}) < P(\text{cause 2} \mid \text{effect}),$$

once you know that the effect occurred, knowing that one cause occurred reduces the probability of the other cause. The two causes become dependent. This is known as *explaining away* because it reflects the fact that, if you know that an effect occurred, having one explanation for it in hand (knowing one cause occurred) makes another unrelated explanation for the effect redundant, so it becomes less likely.

People are sensitive to this relation among explanations for an effect, at least in explaining behavior. The social psychology literature reports many examples of *discounting*.[10] That literature focuses on people's explanations of other people's behavior. When you see someone do something, do you attribute their behavior to their personality or to the environment in which they are operating? Imagine that a person says something nice to you. If it's a stranger with nothing to gain, you might be more likely to attribute their behavior to their natural disposition, whereas if it's someone trying to sell you something, I'd recommend being a little more cynical and considering the possibility that salesmanship has something to do with their behavior. They are driven by the selling context.

Westerners tend to attribute behavior to an individual's disposition and not to the situation. The most celebrated instance is Jones and Harris's 1967 study. Participants read pro- or anti-Castro essays written by students. Some participants were told that the students were told what to write; others were told that students chose their own position. Participants then judged the essay writer as pro- or anti-Castro. Judgments tended to conform to the essay; attributions were to people's beliefs rather than to the situation. More relevant to us, Jones and Harris also found explanation discounting. They found that judgments were attenuated when the student had been told to write the essay. The presence of a situational explanation (what the students were told to do) attenuated the preferred dispositional attribution (their attitude to Castro).

In sum, explanation discounting is justifiable, and it's something that people seem to do. But its justifiability derives from the structure of the relevant causal model. In the experiment described, the underlying causal model was causal structure 1.

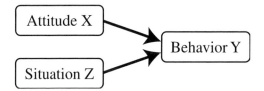

Figure 6.3

Explanation discounting reflects the difference between two judgments: first, the degree-of-belief that an individual is behaving as they do by virtue of their dispositions or attitude:

P(attitude X | behavior Y)

and, second, the degree-of-belief that the person has such an attitude given that you also know of some situation Z, which serves as a causal explanation for their behavior:

P(attitude X | behavior Y, situation Z).

If the attitudinal and situational causes of the behavior are independent, as they are in causal structure 1, in analogy to the paranoia diagram, then explaining away predicts that this second probability should be lower than the first, in line with the phenomenon of discounting. But if the causes are dependent, then this prediction does not necessarily hold. For example, if the underlying causal model is causal structure 2:

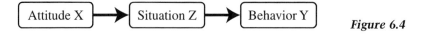

Figure 6.4

the attitude (dispositional) and situational causes should be correlated. Let's assume that causes increase the probability of their direct effects so that, according to causal structure 2, having attitude X increases the probability of situation Z, and situation Z increases the probability of behavior Y. In that case, causal structure 2 also implies that knowledge that situation Z holds should *increase* belief that the individual has the requisite attitude X (and knowing the person has attitude X should also increase belief in the situational explanation). In other words, if the dispositional and situational explanations are believed to be causally related, as they are in causal structure 2, as opposed to independent, as they are in causal structure 1, then we no longer expect discounting to occur.[11]

Here's a little demonstration that discounting depends on the causal model that governs the situation. I told a group of people about tardy Laura:

> Laura is sometimes late for her weekly tae kwon do session. Her instructor has noticed that, when she is late, it is due to either of two unrelated causes: Laura gets extremely stressed at work or Laura gets caught in traffic. When Laura gets extremely stressed, she decides to work later than she has to and therefore arrives late to tae kwon do. When Laura gets caught in traffic, she's late for tae kwon do.

So Laura's tardiness conforms to the causal structure that explains discounting, two independent causes (stress and traffic) and one effect (tardiness). Then I asked half of the group, on a 0–100 scale: "Laura was late for tae kwon do last week. How likely is it that she was extremely stressed?" The other half of the group was also told that she got caught in traffic: "Laura was late for tae kwon do last week. She got caught in traffic. How likely is it that she was extremely stressed?" The first group gave a mean likelihood judgment of 56. The second group discounted her stress because they could explain her tardiness by the amount of traffic. Their mean judgment was only 44. So far, I've replicated the discounting effect that has been repeatedly observed.

But here's a case given to a different group where we don't expect discounting because the story is different. It describes a chain of causes from stress to traffic to tardiness; causes are no longer independent:

> Laura is sometimes late for her weekly tae kwon do session. Her instructor has noticed that, when she is late, it's almost always due to a specific sequence of events: Laura gets extremely stressed at work and then she gets caught in traffic. When Laura gets extremely stressed, she works later than she has to. When she works late, Laura gets caught in rush-hour traffic (which she misses when she works her normal shift), and then she's late for tae kwon do. Other factors may make her late for tae kwon do, but, usually, Laura's lateness is due to the factors just described.

In this case, the discounting effect did not occur. The half of the group that was not told that Laura got caught in traffic, only that she was late for tae kwon do, gave a mean judgment of the likelihood that she was stressed of 81. The half that was told that Laura did get caught in traffic gave a mean stress judgment of 85; they did not discount stress as a factor because, in this case, due to the structure of the causal model, getting caught in traffic made it more likely that she was stressed, not less. Of course, both stress judgments were higher than corresponding judgments with independent causes because in this scenario there was only one causal path to Laura's tardiness, both involving stress, whereas there were two competing causal paths in the first case.

The general lesson is that our confidence in our explanations depends not only on whether those explanations provide a plausible account of the facts. And considering what other explanations are available isn't good enough either. We have to—and we generally do—also consider how explanations relate to one another in a causal model.

Counterfactual Reasoning:
The Logic of Doing

The *do* operator is the key ingredient distinguishing the logic of intervention as embodied by the causal modeling framework from other kinds of logic. This concept distinguishes observation from intervention and gives the framework the ability to represent both action (intervention in the world) and imagination (intervention in the mind). The *do* operator makes a distinct claim about the structure of reasoning, a claim that separates it from standard probability and logical systems. It claims that effects are not always diagnostic of their causes; knowing whether an effect occurred does not always give a clue about whether its normal cause occurred or not. In particular, when an effect is physically or mentally manipulated, it gives no information about its normal causes.

To see this, consider the following causal scenario:[12]

All rocketships have two components, A and B. Movement of component A causes component B to move. In other words, if A, then B. Both are moving.

1. Suppose component A were prevented from moving, would component B still be moving?

2. Suppose component B were prevented from moving, would component A still be moving?

The simple causal model underlying this scenario looks like this:

Figure 6.5

The causal modeling framework represents each question using the *do* operator because each involves intervention; an outside agent is preventing one of the components from moving. We can represent each question, respectively, in terms of *do*(Component does not move):

1. P(Component B moves | *do*(Component A does not move))
2. P(Component A moves | *do*(Component B does not move)).

To evaluate these entities, we must assume (obviously) that the component prevented from moving does not in fact move. According to *do* logic (see chapter 5), we must also simplify the causal model by removing any links into the prevented component (because we are setting its value, its causes are not). This has no effect when A is prevented because A has no normal causes. And because A's links to its effects remain operative, A's movement still determines B's. Hence, if A is not moving, B shouldn't be either, and the answer to the first question should be "no." This is what the vast majority of people say.

But when B is prevented, we must disconnect it from A:

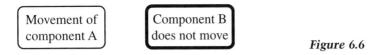

Figure 6.6

As there is no longer any linkage between the components, it is apparent that component A's movement is now independent of B's movement, and therefore the causal modeling framework predicts the *undoing effect*, that component B's lack of movement is not diagnostic (it is uninformative) of its normal cause, A. In other words, people should infer that A would still be moving and respond "yes" to the second question. Again, this is what most people say.

The undoing effect is directly contrary to the prediction of any theory based on probability that does not distinguish intervention from observation, that is, a theory that does not have the *do* operator (or its equivalent) at its disposal. Such a theory might use a standard conditional probability to model the questions. That is, it would ask what the probability is that the components would move given that we *observe* that a component does not move:

> 1'. P(Component B moves | Component A does not move)
> 2'. P(Component A moves | Component B does not move).

In fact, (1) and (1') turn out to be identical. Whether we observe component A not moving or whether it is prevented from moving by external intervention, the link from A to B remains, and therefore the probability that component B moves is the same. However, (2) and (2') are quite different. I just argued that (2) should be high because the linkage from A to B is removed by the *do* operation when B is prevented from moving. In contrast, (2') should be low. It reflects the observational probability of A moving if B does not and must be ascertained using the original causal graph in which A and B are connected. In the normal course of events, A does not move when B doesn't, and therefore people should answer "no."

This analysis predicts that people should answer "no" to both questions when the components are observed not to move, as opposed to being intervened on. To find out, we can see how people answer questions about observation:

> 1. Suppose component A were observed not to be moving, would component B still be moving?
> 2. Suppose component B were observed not to be moving, would component A still be moving?

As predicted, people tend to respond "no" to both questions.[13] Any theory that does not distinguish observation from intervention is unable to explain why people give different answers when the components are observed rather than intervened on.

Like conventional probability theories, conventional propositional logic (the kind taught in elementary logic textbooks) does not make this distinction. A conventional logical analysis of the prevention problem might use the following argument. The problem tells us that if component A moves, then component B moves. We know that B does not move (because it's being prevented from moving). Logic allows one to derive from this that A does not move either. In brief:

If A, then B.
Not B (i.e., B does not move).
Therefore, not A (i.e., A does not move).

This is a conventional argument form known as *modus tollens*. It states that people should conclude "no, component A does not move" whether B is prevented from, or observed not to be, moving. But as we've seen, that's not what people say. If B is prevented from moving, A can move just as well. In the realm of observation, modus tollens is a perfectly valid form of argument if you think that conclusions can be derived with certainty and not merely with probability. But in the realm of action/intervention, and to be in such a realm implies that we're talking about causality, modus tollens isn't necessarily valid because we have to break the link between the first and second parts of the if-then statement when we're intervening on the second part. This is one important limitation of textbook logic, that it has no means of expressing counterfactual actions like "if B had not moved."

If the problem concerns logical if-then relations instead of causal ones, then modus tollens may well be appropriate, and people should use it to derive an answer of "no" to the first question. And indeed they are more likely to, although they seem to be much more confused in a logical than in a causal context in that their answers are more wide ranging and they often express less confidence.[14] People's discomfort with logical problems relative to causal ones arises either because there are different forms of logic and it's not clear which one to pick or because no form of deductive logic comes naturally to us.

Conclusion

The studies reviewed in this chapter are a sampling of the psychological literature showing how causal considerations enter into people's reasoning. Their existence increases my degree-of-belief that people are natural causal reasoners. We easily understand at least simple causal structures and reason about them rationally, showing sensitivity to both explaining away and the logic of intervention.

The examples of reasoning discussed in this chapter all concern qualitative, as opposed to quantitative, knowledge. For example, the work on understanding mathematical equations shows that people can identify causes and effects and use that knowledge to qualitatively order variables in an equation, to decide which variable gets isolated on one side of the equal sign and which variables go together on the other side. It does not show that people have a solid understanding of the precise quantitative relations among the variables, and most people probably don't.

A lot can be accomplished by purely qualitative reasoning. Indeed, reasoning qualitatively can be more efficient than quantitative reasoning because it can simplify computation and can sometimes work when there are not enough data to support a full quantitative analysis. For instance, if you're trying to cross a street, it's enough to know that an oncoming car is speeding up to convince you to stop and wait; you don't need to know the car's precise acceleration. The study of qualitative reasoning has opened an important area of artificial intelligence.[15] Its aim is to understand how to reason about continuous properties of the physical world, like space, time, and energy, in qualitative terms. This area has the potential to provide deep insights into how people reason about the physical world by specifying in detail what a normal person's causal model might look like.[16]

Different logics apply to different situations. Causal logic applies to causal reasoning, deontic logic to reasoning about permission and obligation, arithmetic to relations among magnitudes, and so on. But only some kinds of logic seem to be natural, that is, built into the human reasoning system by evolution or creation. I've argued in this chapter that causal reasoning is natural in this sense. Other kinds of logic may be natural when reasoning about other kinds of situations that don't involve causal relations.[17] But some kinds of inferences require a course in logic to master, and even then they are often not mastered. Textbooks on logic are full of examples. The study of reasoning is in large part figuring out which kinds of logic are natural and which aren't.

7

Decision Making via Causal Consequences

People with yellow teeth are more likely to have lung cancer than people with white teeth. Would you therefore recommend to someone who is worried about lung cancer that they should have their teeth whitened? Probably not.[1]

Whitening teeth would make sense if tooth color were a cause of lung cancer.

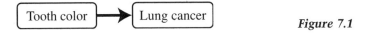

Figure 7.1

But the reason why yellow teeth and lung cancer are correlated is presumably not that one is a cause of the other. It's rather that both are effects of smoking.

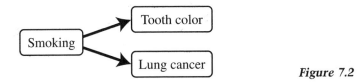

Figure 7.2

Whitening teeth would merely get rid of one effect, yellow teeth, without getting at the underlying cause, smoking, and thus would do nothing to counteract the target effect, lung cancer. Whitening

teeth would be an action by an agent that would constitute an
intervention. According to the logic of intervention (as embodied
by the *do* operator, see chapter 5), the right way to represent intervention in this case is by disconnecting tooth color from its
normal cause (the model shows only one of them, smoking:

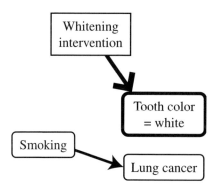

Figure 7.3

Therefore, the intervention would render tooth color independent of
smoking and, in turn, of lung cancer. Whitening would have no
effect on the likelihood of getting lung cancer. It would be a classic
case of curing the symptom while ignoring the problem. Certain
psychoactive drugs have this property. They mask a symptom (like
pain or anxiety) without affecting its cause. This can be dangerous if
the cause has other detrimental effects.

These examples illustrate the logic of intervention with causal
models in decision making. Decision making is one of the most
critical activities that people engage in, suggesting again how important causal models are to human thought.

Making Decisions

We've made a decision whenever we've chosen one or more options
from a set of available alternatives. We make big decisions that can
affect how long we live (like whether to smoke); we make decisions
that determine whether other people live (whether to use birth
control, whether to hit the brakes in the face of oncoming traffic,
whether to drive after that 5th birthday toast) and, if we're powerful
enough, what kind of world future generations will inherit (one
with or without affirmative action, abortion, global warming, etc.).

We also make little decisions like whether to sit down, whether to change lanes, whether to take our keys out of our pocket. In a sense, life is composed of a series of decisions. Of course, we're not aware of all the decisions we make, but they nevertheless are made.

Economics and ethics, as well as areas of psychology, political science, the law, business, sociology, and other fields are concerned with how people make decisions. Some fields, like political science, are more interested in how groups of people make decisions. Economists tend to be more interested in the big picture that emerges when many people are making lots of little decisions. These are the kinds of processes that drive inflation, unemployment, and the Dow-Jones industrial average. They are all aggregate measures of a huge number of individual events of buying, selling, hiring, and firing. In contrast, psychologists and cognitive scientists tend to be more interested in how individuals make decisions.

Everyone who studies decision making has two concerns. One is how decisions are, in fact, made. This is often referred to as a *descriptive* enterprise because it involves describing the actual process of decision making. The other is how decisions *should* be made. This is often referred to as a *normative* enterprise. It concerns the best way for a decision maker to achieve their own goals, what the optimal set of choices is given what you want. To illustrate, a descriptive theory of smoking would list the factors that cause people to smoke (enjoyment, desire to be cool, etc.) and the effects of smoking (yellow teeth, lung cancer, a thinner wallet, etc.) without any value judgment. A normative theory would assess how well smoking serves to achieve one's goals. If one's goal is to maximize pleasure without concern for the future and you enjoy smoking, then a good normative theory would prescribe smoking. One definition of rationality is behaving in a way that is consistent with the best available normative theory; irrationality is behaving at odds with the best available normative theory.[2]

The Gambling Metaphor: Expected Utility Theory

The study of decision making has been dominated by the gambling metaphor. The rational decision maker has been thought of as someone playing a game like roulette in which there are a set of possible outcomes, each with some probability of occurring and each with some value (or *utility*) for the decision maker. The best options are the ones that have, on average, the highest likelihoods of delivering the most stuff. More precisely, the best options are the ones with the highest *expected utility*. Hence, expected utility theory is often treated as the best available normative theory of decision making, especially by economists and sometimes by philosophers.

To make the notion of expected utility concrete, let's illustrate it with some simple calculations. In American roulette, a ball is spun on a round wheel. When the spinning stops, the ball comes to rest in one of 38 numbered slots (0, 00, and 1–36). The object of the game is to predict which number or numbers the ball will land on. Various bets are allowed. Let's say you're deciding between (1) a one number bet (a *straight up* bet) in which you win if the ball lands on your number and (2) an *even* bet in which you win if the ball lands on any even number (you lose if the ball lands on 0 or 00). If you bet straight up, the probability of winning is only 1 in 38 (.0263), but if you win, you're paid 35 times your bet. If you make an even bet, the probability of winning is 18/38 (.4737), but a winner is paid only an amount equal to the amount bet. Say you have $100 to bet and your spouse is nagging you that it's 4 AM and time to go home, so you have time for only one more bet. Which bet do you choose, straight up or even?

The expected utility answer depends on the probabilities of winning, the amounts you might win, and how much you value the win amounts. The value you place on the various amounts you can win is known as your utility function for money. If you bet straight up, there's a small chance you'll win $35 \times \$100 = \$3500$. If you bet even, you're more likely to win, but the most you can win is $100. To most gamblers, winning $3500 is better than winning $100. Is it 35 times better? That depends on your utility function. For many people, it will be less than 35 times better (although if you have a car payment of $3499 due tomorrow and you'll lose your car if you don't pay it, it might be worth more). Let's say that for you it's 30 times better. In that case, we can say that, for you today for this choice, the utility of $100, which I'll write as U($100), is 100 utils, where a util is a completely arbitrary unit of how much you value things that's useful for comparing how much you value different things. The utility of $3500, U($3500), is 3000 utils because 3000 utils $= 30 \times 100$ utils.

What are the two bets worth? Expected utility theory assumes that the value of a bet is the expected number of utils you'll come away with. The expected utility of both bets is the probability of losing times the value of losing the bet amount ($100) plus the probability of winning times the value of winning. Let's assume that the value to you of losing $100 is -100 utils. For a straight up bet, the expected utility is then

$$(1-.0263) \times -100 \text{ utils} + .0263 \times 3000 \text{ utils} = -18.47 \text{ utils}.$$

For an even bet, it's

$$(1-.4737) \times -100 \text{ utils} + .4737 \times 100 \text{ utils} = -5.26 \text{ utils}.$$

Therefore, if these are your utilities, you should take an even bet rather than a straight up bet because the even bet has a less negative expected value. However, because the expected utilities of both bets came out negative, the real prescription of expected utility theory in this case is that you shouldn't bet at all. You're more likely to come out feeling bad than feeling good. Just walk out. That would have the additional positive consequence of pleasing your spouse even more.

Expected utility analyses don't apply only to decisions about money. If you're deciding where to go on vacation, the theory supposes you should consider each option (Hawaii, Las Vegas, North Dakota—whatever suits your fancy). For each option, you should spell out all the possible outcomes (e.g., you go to Las Vegas and win the jackpot versus you go to Las Vegas, spend your last dime, get thrown out of your hotel room, get picked up for vagrancy, etc.). Next, for each possible outcome, you should estimate the probability that it will occur and how good or bad such an outcome would be (the outcome's utility). Finally, for each option, use the probabilities and utilities to calculate its expected utility (multiply the probability of each outcome by its utility and add together all the products). By choosing the option with the highest expected utility, then in the long run you'll get the most utility (which is, by definition, what you want).

This utilitarian view of decision making effectively characterizes much normative behavior. In some special cases, it even effectively characterizes actual behavior.[3] However, as we'll see later in this chapter, it leads to some paradoxical claims about rational behavior and thus seems to miss something at a normative level. It also fails to predict a lot of actual decision making and thus is inadequate descriptively. Some of these failures, both normative and descriptive, have to do with the fact that it ignores causal models. In particular, it fails to appreciate that a decision is really an intervention. Choosing an option from a set is an action that can be represented only with the logic of intervention (or its equivalent).

Deciding by Causal Explanation

It shouldn't be a surprise that causal models are fundamental to decision making.[4] After all, how do we know the outcomes of the options we choose? Outcomes are causal consequences, and one of the causes of outcomes is choice. In choosing a vacation spot, the outcomes (how much we enjoy ourselves, how much we learn, who we meet, etc.) are a consequence of our choice (the outcomes will be different depending on whether we go to Hawaii or North Dakota, etc.

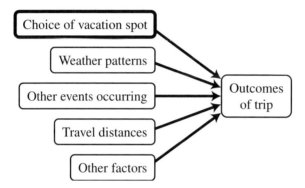

Figure 7.4

The outcomes also depend on how the weather is in the various places, what festivals and other events are occurring, what the trip is like getting there, as well as many other factors. Of course, the one we control, the choice of spot, is critical. How the other factors influence our vacation will depend on our choice. If we choose to go to North Dakota, then the weather in Hawaii will not matter.

Who would want to make a decision, especially an important one, without first understanding the situation surrounding the choice? And it's long been known that the way humans understand is by representing what causes what. Some of the classic work on how people remember stories, by Sir Frederick Bartlett, shows that people fill in gaps by using causal schema that they have acquired through their personal experience. Indeed, people have difficulty understanding a story when the events are inconsistent with their view of how the world works.[5]

Causal structure also influences the impact of facts on our decisions. Causally relevant facts have more influence than causally irrelevant ones. Nancy Pennington and Reid Hastie asked students to pretend to be members of a jury in a criminal case.[6] They presented evidence to these mock jurors and asked them to decide whether an accused person was guilty of murder. Half the jurors received the evidence in the form of a causal story. For these jurors, the events were described according to chronological sequence, and every action had a reason. The other half of the jurors saw exactly the same evidence, but not in the form of a story. For these jurors, the evidence was presented in an arbitrary order like the order that a series of witnesses who saw different parts of the storyline might present it in.

The results were clear. Jurors were persuaded more by evidence that was presented in the form of a causal story than the same evidence presented in arbitrary order. If the causal story had murder as an outcome, then jurors were more likely to convict the defendant, and if the causal story had self-defense as an outcome, then the jurors were more likely to acquit. Strong evidence per se does not automatically lead people to conclude guilt; the evidence must sustain an explanation. The best support for an explanation comes from a plausible causal model.

These studies suggest that, at least in some cases, the trick to persuading someone that an event occurred is to provide them with a causal model that explains how the event is the natural outcome of events that are known to have occurred. A causal explanation can be an effective means of persuasion. Other research shows that an even better way to convince someone is to give them the resources that will allow them to generate the explanation themselves.[7] The best way to convince someone is to allow them to convince themselves because people are very good at generating causal models. And the presence of a good causal model can make any decision much easier.

Newcomb's Paradox: Causal Trumps Evidential Expected Utility

Now let's turn to one of the paradoxes of expected utility theory. In 1969, Robert Nozick discussed the following problem posed by physicist William Newcomb:[8]

> You have great confidence in a particular demon's ability to predict your choices. This demon is going to predict your choice in the following situation. There are two boxes, a transparent one that contains $1000 and an opaque one that contains either $1,000,000 or nothing. You know (and the demon knows you know, and you know the demon knows, etc.) that if the demon predicts you will take what is in both

boxes, he will put nothing in the opaque box. But if the demon predicts that you will choose only the opaque box, he puts the $1,000,000 in it. You get to choose to be greedy by taking what is in both boxes or shrewd by taking only what is in the opaque box. First, the demon makes his prediction, then he puts the money in the opaque box or not based on his prediction (you don't get to see whether he does or not), then you make your choice.

Should you be greedy or shrewd?

Table 7.1 summarizes each option and its possible outcomes:

The paradox for expected utility theory is that it dictates that the rational choice is to be shrewd. But the obvious thing to do is to be greedy. Right? After all, you're making your choice after the money has or has not been put in the box. So your choice doesn't affect whether the money is there. If the demon put the money there, you do better by choosing both boxes (you get $1,001,000 instead of just $1,000,000), and if the demon didn't put the money there, you do better by choosing both boxes (you get $1,000 instead of nothing). You do better by being greedy regardless of what the demon does; being greedy *dominates* being shrewd. So be greedy. In this (rather unusual) case, greed is preferable.

This isn't what expected utility theory dictates. It says to calculate the expected utility of being shrewd and the expected utility of being greedy and to choose the one with the higher result. The expected utility of being shrewd is the probability of getting $1,000,000 times the value to you of $1,000,000 plus the probability of getting $0 times the value to you of $0. The problem assumes that if you choose only the opaque box, then the probability is high that the demon will predict you'll choose only the opaque box. So you're very likely to end up with $1,000,000 and therefore the expected utility of being shrewd is high.

Table 7.1 Choosing in Newcomb's Paradox

	Money gained	
	Demon predicts choice of opaque box	*Demon predicts choice of both boxes*
Shrewd option: You choose only the opaque box	$1,000,000	$0
Greedy option: You choose both boxes	$1,001,000	$1,000

In contrast, the expected utility of being greedy is much lower. It's the probability of getting $1,001,000 times the value to you of $1,001,000 plus the probability of getting $1,000 times the value to you of $1,000. But the problem supposes that if you choose both boxes, then the probability is high that the demon will predict you'll choose both boxes and you'll be likely to end up with a mere $1,000. So, as long as $1,000,000 is worth a lot more to you than $1,000, the expected value of being shrewd is higher than that of being greedy. So be shrewd.

Expected utility theory seems to have it wrong because, as Nozick pointed out, it doesn't take into account a causal analysis of the situation. It doesn't take into account the fact that your choice comes after the demon is already committed. Here's a causal model of the situation:

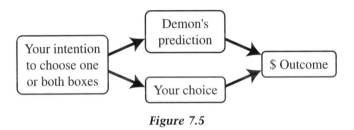

Figure 7.5

Both your choice and the demon's prediction depend on your initial intention to choose one or both boxes. The outcome depends both on what you choose and on the demon's prediction. So far, so good. But here's what expected utility theory misses. Once you actually choose, you've intervened on the world. You've set your choice to one or to both boxes, and thus you have to disconnect it from its normal causes. In other words, the *do* operation (see chapter 5) kicks in.[9] If you choose both boxes, that should be represented as *do* (your choice = both boxes), and the relevant causal model becomes:

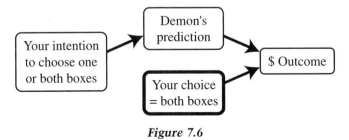

Figure 7.6

Hence, your choice no longer reveals anything about the demon's prediction because it's now disconnected from your initial intention, which was the mediating variable. Because your choice has no bearing on the demon's prediction (that prediction has already been made), the probability that the demon predicts you choose one box or two is no longer relevant. That probability may reveal your initial intentions, but it doesn't relate to your actions. So go ahead and choose both boxes. Whatever the demon predicted, you'll do better. (Of course, if the demon is capable of backwards causality such that its prediction *is* affected by your choice, then all bets are off. But in that case, the problem is purely in the philosopher's domain and can't reveal anything about decision making in the real world. One thing I will bet on is that in the real world causes do not follow their effects.)

The prescription to choose both boxes seems to accord with common sense better than expected utility theory's prescription to choose based on the probability of the demon predicting one box or two. But we really need to be more careful than I have been so far. The causal model framework isn't really at odds with expected utility theory. The problem with the reasoning that I attributed to expected utility theory has to do with the probabilities I used. I said that the problem supposes that if you choose only the opaque box, then the probability is high that the demon will predict you'll choose only the opaque box, and that if you choose both boxes, then the probability is high that the demon will predict you'll choose both boxes. A causal analysis denies that this is true.

The causal analysis proposes that, because your choice is not a cause of the prediction (indeed, it comes *after* the prediction), it cannot affect the prediction, and therefore the demon's prediction has no causal consequences for your choice. All that remains between the demon's prediction and your choice is an evidential relation. Because your choice is influenced by your previous intentions, it provides evidence about those intentions. Given that the demon was able to read your previous intentions, those intentions determined his prediction. Therefore, your choice provides evidence about the demon's prediction. But this evidential relation is irrelevant for choice. Only the causal relation matters.

So all we really need to do to fix expected utility theory is to use probabilities derived from the causal model instead of the probabilities given by the problem. The probabilities from the problem reflect how much evidence your choice provides for the demon's predictions (lots) and therefore we can call them *evidential* probabilities. The probabilities from the causal analysis reflect how much influence your choice has on the demon's predictions when your choice is construed as an intervention. Therefore, we call them *interventional* probabilities. Evidential probabilities come from construing choice as an observation rather than an intervention.

The interventional probabilities tell us that, at the time of choice, the probability of the opaque box containing $1,000,000 if you choose both boxes is the same as the probability of the opaque box containing $1,000,000 if you choose only the opaque box. So if ever you find yourself in this situation, be greedy, and choose both boxes.

Expected utility theory gets the problem right if its prescription is based on interventional rather than evidential probabilities. Nozick called this an argument for causal expected utility theory over evidential expected utility theory.[10]

The Facts: People Care About Causal Structure

Causal structure isn't of interest only to philosophers worried about demons. As the yellow teeth example at the beginning of the chapter shows, everyday decision making is also highly sensitive to the causal relation between choice and outcome.

Doing the Chores

York Hagmayer and I have shown how sensitive people are to causal structure using the following problem:

> Recent research has shown that of 100 men who help with the chores, 82 are in good health, whereas only 32 of 100 men who do not help with the chores are.
>
> Imagine a friend of yours is married and is concerned about his health. He read about the research and asks for your advice on whether he should start to do chores or not to improve his health. What is your recommendation? Should he start to do the chores or not?

Clearly there are plenty of good reasons for doing the chores (for one, it could be crucial to his marriage). But if your friend's main concern is his health, then it's not clear what to recommend in this case. Knowing that there's a correlation between doing the chores and good health—that men who do the chores tend to be more healthy than men who don't—isn't enough. This correlation might arise because doing the chores causes men to be more healthy, or because being healthy causes men to do chores, or because doing the chores and being healthy are both effects of some third variable. Whether doing the chores will improve health depends very much on why the two are correlated, so a wise decision maker should want to know the reasons why doing the chores and being healthy go together.

To disambiguate the possible reasons, we added one of two causal explanations to the problem. Half the participants were told the following:

> Recent research has shown that of 100 men who help with the chores, 82 are in good health, whereas only 32 of 100 men who do not help with the chores are. The research also discovered that the cause of this finding was that doing the chores is an additional exercise every day and therefore improves health.

In other words, the following *direct cause* model was suggested to this group:

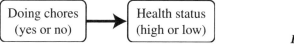

Figure 7.7

According to this causal model, doing the chores is a direct cause of health status, and therefore taking up the chores would indeed improve one's health. Hence, it's recommended.

Another group was given a different causal model, a *common cause*. These participants were told:

> Recent research has shown that of 100 men who help with the chores, 82 are in good health, whereas only 32 of 100 men who do not help with the chores are. The research also discovered that the cause of this finding was that men who are concerned about equality issues are also concerned about health issues and therefore both help to do the chores and eat healthier food.

In other words, this causal model was suggested:

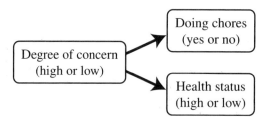

Figure 7.8

According to this causal model, degree of concern is a common cause of both doing the chores and health status, which are not causes of one another. Choosing to do the chores is an action by an agent that sets a variable to a value and is therefore an intervention, so it should be represented with the *do* operation: *do*(Doing chores = yes). This results in a new causal model:

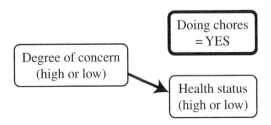

Figure 7.9

Doing the chores is now disconnected from degree of concern and from health status. It affects neither. Therefore, health is not improved by doing the chores, so health status does not provide an additional reason to do the chores.

People's recommendations turned out to be consistent with the causal analyses. Even though the correlation between doing the chores and health was identical in the two cases—the *evidential* relation was the same, about 3 times as many people recommended doing the chores when it was a direct cause of health status than when they were both common effects of degree of concern—the *causal* relations were different. This suggests that people are attuned to the causal consequences of their actions.

Marketing: Bringing Newcomb's Paradox Down to Earth

Hagmayer and I also demonstrated the importance of causal structure to an everyday kind of decision using a problem with a logic similar—not identical—to that of Newcomb's paradox. I've highlighted the causal information by putting it in bold (it was not in bold in the actual experiment):

> Imagine that you are responsible for marketing at a U.S. car manufacturer. You have prepared a marketing campaign for your Minivan "Boston" and your Sedan "Atlanta." Your budget allows you to promote only one of these cars, so you should invest in the campaign that will increase sales the most. You have to decide which campaign to launch next week.

Your main competitor is a Japanese company producing a minivan and sedan very similar to yours. **In the past, you and your competitor started campaigns for the same type of car almost every time.** To be more specific, he started a campaign for his minivan 95% of the time you promoted your minivan, and he promoted his sedan 95% of the time you promoted your sedan. Overall, he split his marketing efforts equally between those two types of car.

Currently you do not know which car he will promote; you only know that he has already decided on his campaign and will not be able to change his decision.

You calculated how many cars of each type you will probably sell, depending on you and your competitor's marketing strategy. The table [7.2] shows you the expected number of additional sales.

Based on this information, which campaign will you launch, one for the minivan or one for the sedan?

Like with Newcomb's paradox, two competing principles are at work here. One, evidential expected utility, says that you should calculate how much each option is worth based on the assumption that your competitor will promote the same type of car as you 95% of the time. This implies that you are very likely to end either in the minivan/minivan cell or the sedan/sedan cell. You'll sell 10,000 more cars in the minivan/minivan cell, so you should promote your minivan.

But this strange logic flies in the face of two critical facts. First, whatever he does, you do better if your promote your sedan (if he promotes his minivan, you sell 40,000 additional units by promoting your sedan rather than only 30,000 by promoting your minivan; if he promotes his sedan, you sell 5,000 more additional units by promoting your sedan). Promoting your sedan *dominates* promoting your minivan.

Second, he's already decided on his campaign; your choice has

Table 7.2 Additional Sales Expected

	Additional sales	
	Competitor promotes his minivan	Competitor promotes his sedan
You promote your minivan	30,000	15,000
You promote your sedan	40,000	20,000

no influence on him. We need a causal analysis to represent this situation correctly. Here's a causal model of the situation:

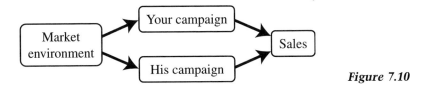

Figure 7.10

You both analyze the market and 95% of the time come to the same conclusion about the best vehicle to promote. Your additional sales are then governed not only by your choice of vehicle to promote but by his as well (because the numbers are different in the two columns). Now, as before, a choice is an intervention. So your choice of campaign should be represented as such. If you choose to market your sedan, *do*(Your campaign = sedan), we have:

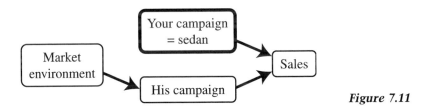

Figure 7.11

Once you've made your choice, it has no implications for the market environment. That is, choosing a campaign strategy tells you nothing about the market environment that you didn't already know. Hence, and more important, choosing a strategy has no influence on his campaign (after all, he's already decided what he's going to try to sell). So you may as well promote your sedan, because you'll sell more cars if you do, no matter what he decides to do.

If the causal structure of the situation were different, then a causal analysis could prescribe a different choice. Imagine that the problem had been written as follows, differing from the first problem only in the bold parts, implying a different causal model:

> Your main competitor is a Japanese company producing a minivan and sedan very similar to yours. **In the past, your competitor has started a campaign for the same type of car after you have started a campaign almost every time.** To be more specific, he started a campaign for his minivan 95% of the time you promoted your minivan, and he

promoted his sedan 95% of the time you promoted your sedan. Overall, he split his marketing efforts equally between those two types of car. **Currently, you know that he has not decided about his campaign.**

Otherwise, the problem is the same as the last one. Now the causal model is:

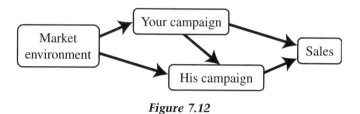

Figure 7.12

In this case, your campaign choice will influence his campaign choice (even after the *do* operation) because an intervention means that we disconnect an event from its causes, not from its effects.

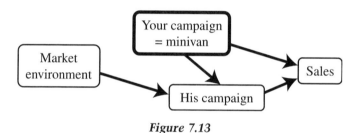

Figure 7.13

So, with probability .95, he'll follow your lead, so you may as well promote your minivan because you'll sell more vehicles if you both promote your minivans than if you both promote your sedans.

What Hagmayer and I have shown is that people's choices on this hypothetical marketing problem depend very much on the causal structure of the situation. Even though the probabilities and sales figures remain the same, people are more willing to promote the sedan under the first causal scenario than the second. Nozick believed that a causal analysis subdued his demon; Hagmayer's less sophisticated participants seem to believe that a causal analysis will subdue the demon of the free market.

When Causal Knowledge Isn't Enough

The evidence that I've reviewed does not show that people's decisions always make causal sense. And in fact they don't. Social psychology is full of counterexamples, cases where people perform actions not to achieve their causal consequences but to convince themselves of the action's normal causal antecedents, because the actions are typical of the kind of person they want to be. We have all had the experience of eating something or listening to something or smoking something not because we enjoyed it but because we felt that if we're a certain kind of person (sophisticated or sensitive or cool), then that's how we would behave. The decision was made not because of the beneficial causal consequences of the action but instead because the action was *diagnostic* of a cause that we wanted to be true.

This kind of decision making verges on self-deception. Consider a study by George Quattrone and Amos Tversky.[11] They told a bunch of Stanford undergraduates that they were studying how rapid changes in temperature affect heart rate after exercise. The students were asked to hold their arms in very cold water for as long as they could. If you've ever done this, you know that it's very painful and that the pain increases over time. The students were then asked to do it again after spending a minute vigorously riding an exercycle. The experimental manipulation was to tell half of the group that people can tolerate cold water for longer after exercise if they have a good type of heart, a type that leads to a longer life expectancy, and to tell the other half the opposite: that people can tolerate cold water for less time if they have the good heart type. What happened is that the group that was told that those with good hearts can last longer did last longer, whereas those told the opposite showed even less tolerance for the cold.

Causally speaking, this just isn't sensible. What they were told can be summarized as follows:

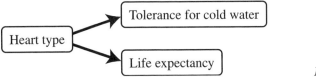

Figure 7.14

So changing their tolerance for cold water wouldn't increase their life expectancy even if they believed the experimenter. But changing their tolerance for cold water was *diagnostic* of having a good heart, which in turn suggested a longer life expectancy. People did not last longer or shorter in the water because of causal consequences, but because it suggested something that they wanted to believe. This is like avoiding heavy clothing when you know you're going to be weighed at the doctor's office. It doesn't make you thinner, but it might make you think you're thinner.

It's possible that in cases like this people either fail to understand the causal contingencies or fail to reason appropriately with them. But another possibility is that they recognize and reason appropriately; they just choose to ignore the causal implications. More precisely, some people might manipulate the outcome (time in cold water or weight at the doctor's office) while simultaneously denying to themselves that they are doing so. After all, if they are not controlling the outcome, then the outcome is indeed diagnostic of the cause they desire (a good heart or to be thin). This is a form of self-deception and is suggested by the fact that most of Quattrone and Tversky's volunteers denied that they had made a conscious effort to tolerate more or less cold, yet their tolerance favored the cause they wanted to be true.

Self-deception isn't necessarily a bad idea. For example, deceiving ourselves into believing we like people more than we do can increase harmony and cooperation. Deceiving ourselves into believing that our vote counts when in fact one vote among millions couldn't possibly make a difference prevents a situation in which nobody bothers to vote (in which case, of course, our vote would count for a lot!).[12] What these examples suggest is that our desire to convince ourselves and others that certain desirable facts are true can lead us to behave in a way inconsistent with the dictates of causal knowledge.

In general, both normative thinking and naïve thinking about decisions always depend on a causal model of the decision situation. However, that causal model doesn't always dictate what people decide. Sometimes people make decisions that reflect how they want the world to be, rather than according to their understanding of how the world actually works. This fact about people is itself a causal mechanism governing one way in which people influence their environments. Behaving as one wants the world to be can make it more likely that the world will actually turn out that way.

8

The Psychology of Judgment: Causality Is Pervasive

Causal models are an extremely effective tool for understanding, predicting, and controlling our environments. They are general purpose; they allow us to represent causal systems of all kinds, be they physical, biological, social, cultural, or purely imaginary. They give us a way to ensure that we're making sense, that the body of beliefs we have and conclusions we come to hang together in a reasonable way. For example, they ensure that we think an effect is likely if all its causes happen to be operating or that a cause is likely if it's the only explanation available for an effect.

In psychology, the test of a theory goes beyond its ability to explain why people behave in reasonable ways, why they behave rationally. After all, people are obviously smart and adaptive (most people, anyway). So the fact that people do something well doesn't necessarily say anything specific about *how* they're doing it, other than to say that they've learned and internalized the demands of the task that they're performing. To see a person do something well means that they've accommodated themselves to the requirements of what they're doing. So the explanation for their behavior—a theory of behavior—has as much to do with what they're doing as it does with the method by which they're doing it. Therefore, the test of a psychology theory should go beyond what people do well and focus also on where people go wrong, on mistakes and error. Because if the theory can predict what kinds of mistakes people make and people indeed make those mistakes, then people must not have truly learned the task they're performing. The failure must concern how they're doing it.

This is obvious when one is studying perception. On a clear night, when the moon is close to the horizon, it looks large, sometimes very large. However, if you measure its actual size on your eyeball (just use a ruler to measure the moon at arm's length), you'll discover it's roughly the same size it is every night. Why? Probably because its proximity to the horizon means that you see things in between you and the moon (trees, houses, etc.), and they give you the impression that the moon is far away. When things are far away, we automatically adjust their size in our minds, making them bigger. You can even test this theory. The next time the moon looks large because it's near the horizon, put your fingers around it, blocking anything on the earth from view. I bet it'll look its normal size. The moon illusion reveals something about how we see. Our visual systems enlarge objects at a distance. We know this by virtue of an error, an illusion. If there were no error, then we'd have to say the moon looks larger because it is larger.

Error opens a window into the workings of the mind not just in perception but in causal modeling as well. In this chapter, we'll see that humans make a variety of judgments that are not quite right; they are biased by our use of causal models. This will provide us with strong evidence for the psychological reality of causal models.

Causal Models as a Psychological Theory: Knowledge Is Qualitative

But first I note an important point. The causal modeling framework in its entirety is not a plausible psychological theory. As I said in chapter 4, the framework has three parts: the world being modeled, a causal graph, and a probability distribution. We know the causal modeling framework is not a perfect model of human reasoning and judgment because we know that people do not always represent probability distributions accurately. This is one of the key conclusions of work by psychologists Amos Tversky and Danny Kahneman, work that Kahneman won the Nobel Prize in economics for in 2001 (Tversky died in 1996, and the prize is awarded only to the living). People cannot be relied on to be accurate judges of probability. We'll see examples of this throughout the rest of this chapter, examples drawn from situations in which people employ causal knowledge.

If people do not have what it takes to make accurate probability judgments always, what remains of causal model theory? Should the theory be discarded in its entirety? One remaining hypothesis is that the structure of causal graphs is an important part of how people represent the world; people represent the *qualitative* structure of causal systems without accurately representing all *quantitative* details. We know what causes what and how things operate in combination to produce effects without knowing exactly how strong the causal relations are. If you think about your knowledge about how a car works, for example, you may know more or less. But you can surely say something about the relations among quite a variety of different components: surely steering wheels, accelerator pedals, keys, wheels, batteries, and perhaps even spark plugs, starter motors, gasoline, combustion chambers, pistons. At a qualitative level, all of you have a reasonable idea about how things fit together at least coarsely. Quantitative knowledge is much harder to come by. How often do spark plugs fail? How much gasoline is required to start an engine? What's the probability that the car will move if you step lightly on the accelerator pedal? To answer the last question, the only response I can give is qualitative. It depends on the weight in the car, the steepness of the grade, whether the car is stuck in mud or sliding on ice.

The idea that people have accurate qualitative knowledge but inaccurate quantitative knowledge is a good first approximation to what people know about causal systems, but it's not entirely accurate. First, people's ability to reason qualitatively is less than perfect. Fischhoff, Slovic, and Lichtenstein presented people with causal models of why a car won't start (they called them "fault trees") that included various alternative systems that could be at fault (battery charge insufficient, starting system defective, etc.), as well as more specific reasons why a system might fail (e.g., the battery charge may be insufficient because of faulty ground connections). The causal models that they presented were either more complete or less complete; that is, they either included most of the reasons a car wouldn't start or they intentionally omitted some reasons. When the experimenters asked people to estimate what proportion of car-starting failures should be blamed on each system, they found that people tended to ignore systems that weren't mentioned in the causal model. People acted as if the only relevant concerns involved systems mentioned by the experimenters, even when the experimenters asked them to consider other reasons why cars might not start that were not mentioned in the causal model.

This experiment suggests that people's qualitative knowledge is imperfect in the sense that we rely heavily on what we're told and tend to ignore qualitative possibilities not mentioned.[1] (There's a lesson here for politicians. If you don't mention a problem, people are likely to ignore it. Of course, effective politicians already know this.)

On the flip side of the qualitative/quantitative divide, we do have access to some quantitative knowledge. We know that stepping harder on the accelerator pedal turns the wheels more than stepping lightly. We know that tires fail more often than steering wheels. A big part of the study of causal models involves understanding how we are able to derive these kinds of quantitative relations in a system that does not maintain precise quantitative knowledge.

The Causality Heuristic and Mental Simulation

Which of the following events is more probable?

- A man has a history of domestic violence if his father has a history of domestic violence.
- A man has a history of domestic violence if his son has a history of domestic violence.

To many people, the first one will seem more probable because it is easy to imagine how a father would causally transmit a tendency to domestic violence to his son, either by role modeling or genetically.[2] But if we're talking about the same man, or two men chosen from equivalent populations, then the two events are in fact equally probable. Knowing the father is guilty may increase the son's probability of guilt, because of the operation of one or another or several causal processes, but those same causal processes imply that the son's guilt increases the probability of the father's guilt. Knowing an effect increases the probability of a cause just as knowing the cause increases the probability of the effect. The effect is *diagnostic* of the cause.

So why does the first statement seem more probable? The answer may be that reasoning about probabilities in this case is harder than reasoning about causality. After all, the thesis of this book is that causal reasoning is easy; it's one of the most natural forms of thinking we engage in. As a result, we interpret the question about probability as a question about causality, as a question like "which statement makes more causal sense?"[3] And in fact, the first statement makes more causal sense because the flow of information is in a causal direction, from cause to effect, rather than from effect to cause. Hence, we give more credence to the first statement even though both statements are equally credible on probabilistic grounds.

Here's another example. Which of the following events is more probable?

- An adult chosen at random from the American population will die of a heart attack within the next 10 years.
- An adult chosen at random from the American population will be obese and will die of a heart attack within the next 10 years.

In problems of this type, many people respond that the second option is more probable than the first.[4] A moment's thought will reveal this is impossible, however, as long as you understand the word *and* to mean that both characteristics are true of the randomly chosen American (the person is obese; also the person will die of a heart attack). The person cannot be more likely to have both characteristics, because if they are obese and will die of a heart attack, then (obviously) it's also true that they will die of a heart attack. So, given that it's also possible that someone who is not obese will die of a heart attack, it's a logical necessity that the first proposition is more probable. Two events cannot be more probable than either one alone. This is called the conjunction rule of probability. Cases in which people's judgments violate the conjunction rule are called *conjunction fallacies*.

Why do people commit conjunction fallacies? In this case, it may again have to do with causal models. Obesity is a well-known cause of heart attacks, so adding obesity to the statement turns it into a causal claim, as if people are judging the probability that a randomly chosen American will die of a heart attack *because* they are obese, even though this is not the question that was asked. And the probability of dying of a heart attack because one is obese may well be higher than the raw probability of dying of a heart attack. In that sense, people may be making a reasonable judgment; they're just not making the judgment they were asked to make. People have a habit of interpreting questions about probability as questions about causality. This suggests that they have the tools to answer questions about causality—causal models—but not always questions about probability.

The role of causal models goes beyond judgments of probability. It affects many kinds of judgment:[5]

Mr. Crane and Mr. Tees were scheduled to leave the airport on different flights, at the same time. They traveled from town in the same limousine, were caught in the same traffic jam, and arrived at the airport

30 minutes after the scheduled departure time of their flights. Mr. Crane is told that his flight left on time. Mr. Tees is told that his flight was delayed and just left 5 minutes ago. Who is more upset, Mr. Crane or Mr. Tees?

Clearly, Mr. Tees, right? He missed his plane by 5 minutes, Mr. Crane by 30. Mr. Tees *almost* caught his flight; Mr. Crane had no chance. It's so easy to imagine another possible world (a counter-factual world) in which Mr. Tees caught his flight. The traffic jam could have been 5 minutes shorter, or Mr. Tees could have left 5 minutes earlier. Imagining a different world in which 30 minutes was saved is much harder. Notice that Mr. Tees's distress has nothing to do with anything he did; he did exactly the same thing as Mr. Crane under exactly the same set of beliefs about the world. The only difference is the way the world *could* have been. The ability to simulate the way the world could have been requires a causal model. Only by running a causal model based on assumptions about the world that happen to be false—counterfactual assumptions like Mr. Tees had left 5 minutes earlier—can one figure out what would have happened in a different world. And not only do we have that ability, we have a habit of doing so even when it does nothing but induce regret and pain.

Belief Perseveration

Causal models are supposedly effective because they accurately portray the way the world is experienced. An individual's causal model is supposed to be grounded in experience; in fact, it is supposed to be a representation of the data generated by experience. But causal models have a habit of taking on a life of their own; they tend to have more influence on judgment than is justified by the facts that they represent. This is obvious in politics where people commonly stick to their causal beliefs regardless of the facts. Politicians, successful ones anyway, have long known not to bother trying to dissuade firm believers with facts. Firm believers are rarely interested in facts; they are interested in perpetuating their causal beliefs, beliefs that may at one time have been based on facts but are no longer tied to them. Failures of the free market are as easily explained by conservatives (as due to "irrational exuberance," say) as failures of the welfare system are by liberals (perhaps as a "bureaucracy out of control"). Both explanations may be right. What's noteworthy (and a little scary) is how easy it is to generate good explanations in support of one's causal beliefs regardless of the facts.

Solid evidence that people behave this way comes from a series of experiments by Lee Ross, Mark Lepper, and their colleagues demonstrating that causal explanations quickly become independent of the data from which they are derived.[6] In one study, they told a group of students about a pair of firefighters, one of whom was successful and also a risk taker, the other unsuccessful and averse to risk. The students were then asked to explain this correlation between performance as a firefighter and risk preference. Why should risk takers be better firefighters? After constructing their explanations, the students were informed that (oops) an error had been made; in fact, the experimenters were confused. In reality it was unknown whether the risk-averse firefighter was more effective; the actual relation between firefighting ability and risk preference was not necessarily the one they had explained. Finally, participants were asked what they really thought. Is it good or bad to be a risk taker if you're a firefighter?

Participants persevered in their beliefs; they continued to assert the relation they had causally explained regardless of the updated information. They said it was better to be a risk taker even though the facts suggested that it was better to avoid risk. Causal beliefs dominate thought and judgment even when they are known to be divorced from the facts. In such cases, causal beliefs can bias our judgment.

Experiments on belief perseverance call for causal explanation. That is, people answer the question "why is it good for firefighters to be risk takers" by explicitly distinguishing causes from effects and stating or implying that the effect would have been different if the cause had been different. Explanations in the physical and social world tend to be causal, but they don't have to be. One could in principle appeal, for instance, to a class inclusion hierarchy (e.g., risk takers are better at everything). But causal explanation is often the most natural form of explanation.

Seeing Causality When It's Not There

One reason that causal models are so central to judgment is that they affect our very perception of events. The Belgian psychologist Albert Michotte (1881–1965) made this point very clearly by presenting participants with dots moving on a screen.[7] When one dot approached the other, touched it, and the other took off, it appeared that the second was causing the first to move even though the motion was apparent, not real. This is not surprising. The entire movie and television industries are built on this perceptual illusion of apparent causality. This is why we see feet kicking balls, hands turning knobs, wheels moving cars, cars chasing other cars (which are chasing helicopters) rather than just a sequence of unrelated objects or even unrelated objects in motion.

We see events in terms of our causal schema. They shape our perception. This can help explain why certain kinds of clinical tests, projective tests like the draw-a-person test or the Rorschach inkblot test, were so popular for so long despite the wealth of data showing that they are useless at predicting personality traits. Consider predictions of male homosexuality using the Rorschach. In the 1960s, Chapman and Chapman studied the matter. The Rorschach consists of a series of standardized cards, each of which contains a blot of ink. People are asked to look at the blot and report what they see. The idea is that, because the inkblot contains no image of anything real, people will project their personality in their interpretation of the image. As we'll see, it turns out that it was the clinicians using the inkblots who were doing the projecting.[8]

Two types of responses to the inkblots are of interest. Type E signs are valid (accurate) predictors of male homosexuality, but there's no obvious reason why they are valid. They are empirically valid, but they lack "face validity." For example, men who see monsters on Card IV or figures that appear to be "part animal" and "part human" on Card V happen to be more likely to be homosexual than people who don't report these signs. The reason is unknown. Type F signs are face valid but empirically invalid. They make sense to people but in fact have nothing to do with whether someone is homosexual or not. They involve seeing anal content, genitalia, feminine clothing, and so forth. In essence, they are the kinds of responses that might be expected from a causal model of what homosexuals would say, a causal model based on prior belief and not on data.

In one study, Chapman and Chapman asked practicing clinicians with many years of experience using the Rorschach to list the five most common responses characteristic of homosexuals. They were all Type F. Only 2 of 32 clinicians ever listed a Type E. Even highly experienced clinicians recalled only responses that conformed to their biased expectations, none that conformed to actual experience. In another study, undergraduates with no experience with projective tests were shown a set of Rorschach cards. Each card indicated a descriptor of a man, either that he was gay ("has sexual feelings toward other men") or something else (e.g., "feels sad and depressed much of the time"). The card also gave a response to the image, either a Type E, a Type F, or some other response. The descriptors and the responses were uncorrelated; each descriptor appeared an equal number of times with each response. In other words, what the individual said about the card had nothing to do with whether they were gay. Next, participants were asked to indicate which symptoms were associated with homosexual descriptors. What did these undergraduates say? Type F, just as the experienced clinicians had done.

Both naïve individuals and experienced therapists saw relations between people and their responses that weren't there. The study itself is a kind of projective test. The participants projected roughly the same expectations about what a homosexual male would say, and then they convinced themselves that this is what homosexual males actually did say, even when they didn't. People's causal models were more powerful instruments of observation and assessment than the world they were actually presented with.

Gilovich, Vallone, and Tversky[9] have shown a similar kind of causal bias among sports fans. They asked basketball fans whether players tend to have "hot hands." More specifically, they said, "Does a player have a better chance of making a shot after having just made his last two or three shots than he does after having just missed his last two or three shots?" In response, 91% of basketball fans said yes. So the researchers examined basketball shooting data to see if the fans were right. The looked at a season's shooting patterns by the Philadelphia 76ers and found no evidence that any player on the team was a streak shooter. They also had college basketball players take free throws from an arc around the basket. Players and spectators both bet on the outcome of each shot. There was no evidence of streaks; players were just as likely to hit their shot if they had just missed a shot as they were if they had just hit their last shot. Nevertheless, both players' and spectators' bets showed they expected streaks. They bet high if the player had made his last shot; they bet low if the player had missed his last shot.

The point here is not that basketball shooting is random. I'd much rather bet on a professional player who shoots 50% from the floor than, say, me, who would be lucky to get 1% of shots if I were able to even get a shot away in the first place, surrounded by superfast giants who would know what I was trying to do before I did. The point has to do with perception. We perceive shooting streaks even when the number of streaks we see can be explained by chance (it's not the hits and misses that can be explained by chance; it's whether one hit depends on another that can be). We expect to see streaks because our causal model tells us that players cannot miss if they are "in the zone," focused, feeling good, relaxed, and so on. This is clear from listening to the play-by-play announcer for just about any game. Announcers are constantly referring to which team is hot, which is cold, which player is playing well, which can't get their mind off yesterday's big loss or their salary negotiation.

We seem to see the game as a series of emotional waves flowing one way and then another, caused by the will and drive of players, coaches, and fans and the skills of the players. And this causal model leads us to expect sequences of shots to follow a pattern, which we then perceive even though it's not there. Blackjack players also report that their luck comes in waves; the key to the game is to surf the swells and avoid the troughs.[10] Perhaps we treat the stock market and the ups and downs of our lives in the same way.

Causal Models and Legal Relevance

Evidence shows that causal models mediate judgments of probability. We can distinguish two types of evidence relevant to making a judgment of the probability of a unique event: evidence about the general type of event (*class* data) and evidence about the specific event itself (*case* data). The distinction is clear in the case of profiling, and so are the legal concerns that arise from the use of class data. Profiling occurs when government officials like the police stop people based on profiles, general descriptions, or class data concerning such characteristics as race, gender, personality, and age without any specific evidence that the individuals have done anything wrong, without any supporting case data. Profiling raises serious concerns because it can lead to detaining innocent people. Nevertheless, class data can be probabilistically very relevant. This might be easier to see in the medical realm. If all you know about someone is their race, then that can help a doctor choose a more likely diagnosis. Races do differ to some extent in their susceptibility to certain diseases. African Americans are 15 times less likely to develop melanoma, a skin cancer, than white Americans. So both class and case data are relevant to judgments of probability. What I'm going to try to show here is that, instead of considering all relevant evidence when making a judgment, people tend to rely on evidence that fits a causal model.

Conventional wisdom, supported by a vast amount of scientific data, tells us that people have a habit of overreliance on class data.

We stereotype. We develop expectations and make judgments about people not based on their individual behavior but on their skin color, their religion, their nationality, or their gender. These stereotypes affect how we see other people. A classic demonstration was offered in 1976 by Condry and Condry. They showed college students a videotape of an infant. Half of the students were told that the infant was a boy, the other half that the infant was a girl. In the videotape, the infant reacted to a jack-in-the-box that suddenly popped open. Students who thought he was a boy interpreted his reaction as anger; those told that she was a girl tended to interpret her reaction as fear. This happened even though they saw the same videotape of the same infant. Apparently class data about a person's gender affect the way we interpret their behavior. Such reactions surely stem in part from our causal beliefs about race, religion, nationality, gender, and so on. At some level, stereotypes are associated with a model of people in which being a boy causes reactions of anger and being a girl causes reactions of fear.

In other situations, just the opposite occurs. Class data are neglected. Tversky and Kahneman argue that when both class and case data are available, case data overwhelm the cognitive field; class data can be treated as background and are therefore neglected. They make the point with the following problem:

> A cab was involved in a hit-and-run accident at night. Two cab companies, the Green and the Blue, operate in the city. Imagine you are given the following information.
>   85% of the cabs in the city are Green and 15% are Blue.
>   A witness identified the cab as a Blue cab. The court tested his ability to identify cabs under the appropriate visibility conditions. When presented with a sample of cabs (half of which were Blue and half of which were Green), the witness made correct identifications in 80% of the cases and erred in 20% of the cases.
>   What is the probability that the cab involved in this accident was Blue rather than Green?

A very common response to this question is .80, the proportion of correct witness identifications. A Bayesian analysis, however, gives a different answer. We must distinguish four variables: W (the witness's report that the cab was blue), B (the event that cab involved in the accident was blue), G (the event that cab was green), and R (the base rate of blue cabs). The question asks for the probability that the cab was blue (B), given the witness's report (W) and that 15% of cabs in the city are blue (R):

$$P(B|W \& R) = \frac{P(W \& B \& R)}{P(W \& R)} \quad \text{according to Bayes' rule (see chapter 5)}$$

$$= \frac{P(W|B \& R) \cdot P(B|R)}{P(W|B \& R) \cdot P(B|R) + P(W|G \& R) \cdot P(G|R)} \quad \text{via a little algebra}$$

$$= \frac{.80 \cdot .15}{.80 \cdot .15 + .20 \cdot .85}$$

$$= .41.$$

On this analysis, the probability that the cab is blue is only about 40%. The cab is more likely to be green than blue despite the witness's report because of the high base rate of green cabs. Yet people's responses indicate that they tend to be guided solely by the witness's report and by the case data, neglecting the class data. The psychologist Ajzen showed a way to get people to consider class data.[11] Tversky and Kahneman in 1982 reported results for a version of the problem in which they replaced the statement of base rates (the second paragraph of the problem) with one that made the base rates appear to be causally relevant to the incident:

> Causal version:
>   Although the two companies are roughly equal in size, 85% of the total accidents in the city involve Green cabs, and 15% involve Blue cabs.

In this case, participants took base rates into some account. They lowered their estimates by roughly .20 on average.

In a causal context like a car accident, one way people could come up with probability estimates is by constructing a causal model and reasoning from it. Apparently, they do not reason about all probabilities. The implication is that evidence—even probabilistically relevant evidence—that is not part of a causal structure can be neglected. The number of cabs in a city isn't *causally* related to the car involved in the accident. It is a set relation. The cab potentially involved in the accident is one of the set of blue cabs in the city. The idea is that we focus on causal relations; hence, we neglect data that is related in other ways.

Such reasoning will not always lead to correct probability judgments but can be justifiable nevertheless. It is generally unfair to blame someone or find them guilty because of their background or their prior conduct. The crimes of your father, or of members of your state or race, even your own previous bad behavior, surely can be informative about the probability of your guilt. But if it is not tied to a specific causal story about the misdeed or accident at hand, it is legally and morally irrelevant. The psychologist Gary Wells showed that people treat "merely statistical" evidence as irrelevant when judging guilt.[12] He used a bus accident scenario closely related to the cab problem except that no case data were reported (i.e., there was no witness). Wells found that even if 90% of buses passing the location of an accident caused by a bus were owned by a certain company, both average people and practicing judges felt that was no basis for a verdict against the company. This is particularly striking given that participants were keenly aware of the relevance of the 90% proportion, in that they knew that the probability that the company was guilty was 90%. Nevertheless, they refused to convict on this basis. Wells points out that legal cases resting on naked statistical evidence of this type are habitually thrown out of court.

To test the hypothesis that the neglect of base rates in the cab problem results from assessments of causal relevance, I ran a small study in which I gave people the cab problem as well as a series of questions intended to reveal their individual causal models of the problem.

The causal model questions asked the participant, for each pair of variables, whether there was a causal relation from one variable to another. For example, to assess the causal relation from the base rate (percentage of green vs. blue cabs) to the judged event (cab involved was green vs. blue), participants were asked if a change in the former would change their belief in the latter. Answers were used to derive a causal model for each participant. To illustrate, someone who responded "yes" only to the question about the effect of a change in the witness's report on belief that the cab was blue would be assigned the witness-only model.

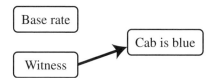

Figure 8.1

This is the simplest model consistent with Tversky and Kahneman's claim that people believe that the witness's credibility was relevant to their judgment but the base rate was not. It was the model most frequently generated. The next most frequent model was the simplest one consistent with the Bayesian response. It showed the relevance to the judgment of both the base rate and the witness's testimony (Bayesian model in fig. 8.2).

No other model was generated with any regularity, although a variety of different causal models was generated. The models can be

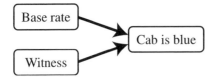

Figure 8.2

divided into two main types using the screening-off property of causal models: those consistent with the witness-only model and those consistent with the Bayesian model.

What I found is that participants who endorsed a witness-only model type were more likely to neglect the base rate, and those who endorsed a Bayesian model type were more likely to give a judgment closer to the Bayesian response that takes both witness and base rate information into account.

Although the restriction to causally relevant evidence has a convincing normative justification in the determination of guilt and blame (one should not be accountable for thy father's sins), morally (and legally) ambiguous cases certainly exist. The issue of profiling is a case in point. Should police be allowed to detain those who fit a racial or ethnic profile for a crime even without direct evidence causally linking the individual to the crime? A profile is purely correlational. It describes probabilistically relevant evidence (perhaps that people with certain facial features are more likely to be terrorists) without regard to the causal basis of the evidence. Detaining someone merely because they fit a profile can be discriminatory and violate individual rights; of course, if the profile is statistically valid, it can also help deter crime. If I'm getting on an airplane, one of my highest priorities is that the plane not be blown up or hijacked by a terrorist. Preventing terrorism requires a focus on the probability that someone is a terrorist, not merely the causal relevance of data. I'd not only feel safer, but I'd be safer if profiles were used to decide who to subject to security checks if resources are too scarce to check everybody carefully, assuming the profiles were accurate. In a decision made soon after the World Trade Center disaster of September 11, 2001, the U.S. secretary of transportation disagreed. He took the moral position that ethnicity must never be a criterion for public judgment.

Conclusion

Causal modeling plays a central role in the process of judgment when the object of judgment can be construed as a causal effect. Such a construal is almost always appropriate in the legal domain where both crimes and accidents are effects of individual actions. It's also appropriate in scientific domains. Scientists are also in the business of building causal models, in their case to understand how the world works in general rather than to understand the circumstances of a specific event. Published work in science doesn't always refer to causation (especially in atomic physics where causation is exceptionally elusive due to the weird probabilistic behavior of atomic particles). However, even hard scientists talk causality all the time in cafés and seminars, if not in their published work.

Causal models are relevant to judgment in any domain in which physical, social, or abstract events cause other events. Causal models may well be the primary determinant of what is considered relevant when reasoning, when making judgments and predictions, and when taking action within such domains.

9

Causality and Conceptual Structure

The world we experience is much richer than the world that impinges on our senses. We see a white sphere with lacing, but we experience a ball, possibly associated with potential actions like throwing and catching, or perhaps associated with memories of a visit to the ballpark or last year's World Series. We see a shape moving across the sky, and we hear a roar, but what we experience is an airplane, knowing that people are on board traveling from one destination to another and potentially inferring much more besides. As Jerome Bruner put it, our experience goes "beyond the information given."[1] Knowledge is brought to bear so quickly and effortlessly to help us interpret objects and events that we're generally unaware just how much of our experience is inferential, made by our own minds and not an unmediated, direct image of the world we're immersed in.

How is this possible? How is our base of knowledge structured to give us such quick and effortless access to what's relevant, despite a sea of information to search through? What is it we know about sets of objects, like balls or airplanes or dogs or people, that allows us to believe and say and even see so much more than is actually present? In other words, what is the nature of conceptual knowledge? What do we know about sets of objects—categories— that allows similar conceptual knowledge to be elicited by very different objects (e.g., we know that both tarantulas and horseshoe

crabs have internal organs)? And how is it that our concepts sometimes make sharp distinctions between similar objects (e.g., French
versus Californian wine or a real Fender Stratocaster electric guitar
versus an imitation)?

Cognitive scientists, and philosophers and psychologists before
them, have had no shortage of ideas about the structure of concepts.
Perhaps the most commonsensical idea is that people construct a
concept to represent all those objects that satisfy some set of logical
conditions, often called necessary and sufficient conditions.[2] Something that is spherical and used to play games is represented by a
concept associated with the word "ball," and, conversely, that concept represents spherical objects used to play games. Well, this idea
didn't last long under the analyses of some clear thinkers and exper-
imentalists.[3] Balls seem a simple case, yet a balloon can be spherical
and can be used to play games (this violates the first part of the definition). Moreover, an American football is a ball, yet it's not spherical
(substitute "rugby ball" for "American football," if you like). This
violates the second part. Maybe the problem is that our definition is
too strict. Maybe a ball is anything used for a game that is sort of round
and tough enough not to break too easily. But this broader definition
leads to its own problems. First, it's not clear how to decide if
something is "sort of round." Moreover, it's still easy to come up with
counterexamples. A hackysack is a bag used for games. It is quite
round and quite tough, yet it's not a ball. And a deflated football isn't
round in any sense, yet it's still a ball. Of course, we could go on and on
trying to arrive at a successful definition (indeed, I challenge you to).
The point is that it's not easy and that we certainly don't have direct
conscious access to necessary and sufficient conditions. Concepts
can't easily be reduced to definitions, and all the evidence suggests
that very few can be at all.

A number of other ideas have been offered to explain how we
decide what knowledge to use when we encounter an object. Here's a
short list. To decide how to categorize an object in front of us, we
judge its similarity to other objects whose categories we know. If it's
most similar to the objects whose category is X, then we judge it an
X.[4] Another theory supposes that each category is associated with a
prototype, a highly representative instance. According to this theory,
we evaluate the similarity of the object to the prototypes that we
know and assign the category of the most similar one.[5] Another
theory assumes that we have an organized body of knowledge associated with each category that specifies why it's important, what
properties or events in the world it's useful for explaining.[6]

All these theories reflect ideas theorists have had about the structure of human concepts, what people know about categories of objects in the world. One property of concepts that any theory must account for is that concepts are flexible because people classify the same set of objects in different ways. Films, for instance, can be classified along many dimensions: production technology (e.g., black-and-white vs. color films), geography (e.g., Hollywood vs. Bollywood films), style (e.g., comedies vs. adventures vs. dramas), financial promise (e.g., blockbuster vs. independent films). Some categories are tied together by abstract features (shot put and running both belong in the track-and-field category at the Olympics); other categories are tied by a common name (teddy bears and grizzly bears are both called "bears"). What objects we select and how we put them together depend on our current goals, the task before us, and on our language and culture. You might argue therefore that concepts are not fixed, stable entities in the mind.[7] Nevertheless, people do bring general knowledge to bear to understand objects and events. This chapter will focus on the structure of that general knowledge, in particular, on its causal structure. The research I present uses a variety of measures of categorization. The most frequent is naming; objects are assumed to belong in the same category if they are called by the same name.

Inference Over Perception

Theories of conceptual structure must explain a ubiquitous finding about how people categorize objects. People don't necessarily categorize an object according to what it looks like; what we can't see can be more important than what we can see. Unobservable properties are often given more weight in a categorization decision than observable properties. For instance, what something does is sometimes extremely important, especially when we're talking about artifacts, human-made objects. An object that can make and receive telephone calls is called a "telephone" whether it looks like what Alexander Graham Bell used, a black box, a miniature racing car, or an object from Star Trek. These days, objects that look just like credit cards are called "keys" because they open doors, usually hotel doors. In both cases, we can talk about the object's function even when the object is not in use, and therefore the function does not directly correspond to anything observable but rather to the object's potential. This potential turns out to be more important to the label we assign the object than anything we are directly observing.

The importance of nonobservable properties has been demonstrated in several ways by researchers. Some of the most provocative demonstrations were reported by Frank Keil.[8] He used natural kinds, object categories not created by people that occur in nature. He told kindergartners, second graders, fourth graders, and adults about a fictitious raccoon that had raccoon parents, raccoon insides, and raccoon genes, but it had been transformed cosmetically to look just like a skunk. It had been given a distinctive odor, a white stripe down its back, and so on. Would you call this strange animal a skunk or a raccoon? Most adults and older kids called it a raccoon because they believed its nonobservable raccoon properties like its insides and its genes were more important for naming it than its observable ones. The fact that it looked like a skunk wasn't judged terribly critical. After all, appearances deceive. Kindergartners weren't governed by this kind of reasoning, however. They tended to call it a skunk.

In Keil's raccoon/skunk example, we're talking about a hypothetical animal. No actual animal in the world is a raccoon on the inside but a skunk on the outside (as far as I know). Because we spend so much of our time talking, dreaming, and arguing about other possible worlds, not just this one (see chapter 3), any theory of concepts better tell us what things are in those other worlds. A concept, in other words, must represent not merely a set of objects in the world but a set of possibilities.[9] Otherwise, there would be no way to explain how we can think about novel instances (like a raccoon that we've never met) or how we are able to analyze counterfactual statements (like "if Stinky were a skunk, he'd have skunk parents"). The set of things that a concept applies to includes real objects that I know about, objects that could exist but I have no knowledge of as yet, like the next skunk that my dog encounters, and even some objects that I believe do not and never will exist, like a raccoon that looks just like a skunk.

The fact that concepts represent both actual and counterfactual objects is reminiscent of causal models. As I discussed in chapter 5, causal models represent both actual and possible events: not only what has happened or is happening, but what will or *could* happen. The close relation between causal models and possible worlds suggests that causal relations might be critical for categorization phenomena like the raccoon/skunk example as well. Indeed, this seems the most natural interpretation of the result. The raccoon/skunk is a raccoon because it has raccoon parents, raccoon insides, and raccoon genes. These properties carry the day because our causal models of animals make these properties causally central.[10] Our causal model of reproduction includes a link equivalent to what we see in figure 9.1.

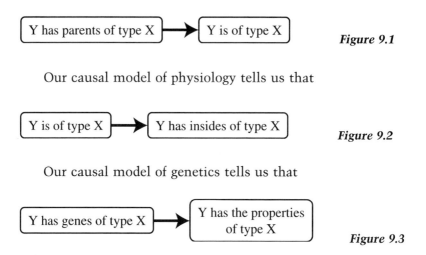

Figure 9.1

Our causal model of physiology tells us that

Figure 9.2

Our causal model of genetics tells us that

Figure 9.3

In sum, all our causal knowledge is consistent with the belief that the raccoon/skunk is actually a raccoon.[11] It might therefore be worth extending the interpretation of causal models that we've considered in previous chapters so that they relate not just events but the properties of objects as well. But before pursuing this line of thought, let's consider some more facts about how people categorize.

The Role of Function in Artifact Categorization

In some experiments, even young children have shown sensitivity to properties that they are not directly perceiving. For example, Kemler Nelson and her colleagues[12] showed preschoolers a simple novel artifact and named it. Then the children had to choose another object that had the same name. They chose between an object similar in function but dissimilar in form and one similar in form but without the function. The children tended to choose objects that preserved the function of the original rather than the form. So any theory of naming must account for the fact that, at least some of the time, what we can't see but must infer is more important than what we can.

One result of Kemler Nelson et al.'s study provides a strong reason to believe that the greater weight given to function over form is due to a causal model. Some of the objects in this experiment were normal artifacts in the sense that the physical structure of the object was obviously designed to perform a particular function, much like a bicycle has a physical appearance (big wheels, pedals, seat a leg's length above the pedals, handlebars at the top in front, etc.) that makes plain that it's designed for humans to ride. Such compatibility between form and function makes it relatively easy to construct a causal model representing a mechanism in which the physical structure is a cause of the function. Other objects in the experiment were odd; they did not appear to be designed to perform their function, like a bicycle with the positions of the handlebars and pedals reversed. It would be hard to construct a causal model for such objects because the mechanism supporting the function cannot be inferred from the physical structure. The results of the experiment showed that the children's preference for preserving function over form when naming was greater for the normal objects than for the odd ones. This suggests that children are more likely to use nonobservable properties to name when those nonobservables can be explained by appealing to a causal model than when such explanation is impossible because no model is available to refer to. The function was important only when its connection to physical structure made sense, suggesting that the connection itself—the causal model—was a critical part of the naming process.

Although Kemler Nelson et al.'s study shows that there are contexts in which the function of an artifact is our overriding concern,[13] there are other contexts in which other features matter more. For instance, Malt and Johnson[14] asked people to name an object made of rubber that provides warmth to the upper body when worn over a shirt. Despite agreeing that this object served the function of a sweater, the participants denied that this object was a sweater. Apparently, people believe that to be a sweater an object requires certain physical properties, like softness. So knowing an object's function is not sufficient for categorization. Malt and Johnson also show that knowledge of function is not necessary for categorization. Sometimes physical features matter more than functional ones. This is more evidence that categorization is flexible. The weight given to different features—functional versus physical in this case—depends on what we're categorizing.

Causal Models of Conceptual Structure

We are looking for a theory that tells us what people know about categories of objects. This theory can't say merely that we categorize things according to their similarity in appearance to other things because we've just seen that hidden properties, like what an object does, its function, can matter more than appearance. And the theory can't be limited to actual objects, because we know about the names of virtual and even some impossible objects. And the theory must accommodate human flexibility: people rely on different features at different times to categorize. In particular, for some objects, people rely on functional properties, and for others, we rely more on physical properties.

A Causal Model of Artifacts

Sergio Chaigneau, Larry Barsalou, and I have suggested such a theory of artifact knowledge.[15] We call it the HIPE theory of function (as opposed to the *hype* theory) because it suggests that an object's function is related to other aspects of the object: its Historical role, the Intentions of an agent using the object, its Physical structure, and the Events that occur when it is used. In the case of artifacts, the events occur when an agent performs an action with an artifact. All these pieces of knowledge are linked via a causal model.

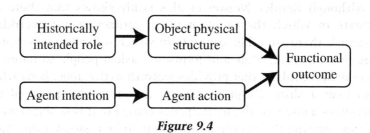

Figure 9.4

The model proposes that people know about four abstract causal relations among these pieces of knowledge. First, an object's historical role causes it to have a certain physical structure because the physical structure of an artifact takes its form from a designer who has given it that form due to its historical role. A car has historically had the role of transporting people and other objects and therefore it has wheels, a passenger compartment, and a trunk; that's why it's big enough to carry people and some objects but not so big that it would be hard to maneuver. Second, an agent's intention causes their actions. A person will press on the accelerator pedal only if they want to go faster. The third and fourth causal relations reflect the direct causes of the functional outcome of an event. On any particular occasion, the function of an artifact is jointly determined by its physical structure and by actions performed by an agent. A car's transportation function is enabled by a driver taking actions on the car's physical parts (e.g., its steering wheel and accelerator pedal) that cause it to move to a destination. So the root causes in this model are the object category's historical role and the intentions of agents using objects in the category. The final effect is what is accomplished by the actions taken on the physical structure. Usually, that's what we think of as the function, although sometimes it's not, like when the car doesn't work.

This theory is intended to summarize a set of general beliefs about artifacts and to provide a framework to explain how people categorize objects. It assumes that category knowledge is complex—it consists of different kinds of knowledge put together in a structured way. Hence, it leads to the expectation that categorization will not always involve one type of feature (physical or functional) but that features' importance will depend on the entire causal model. To be assigned a particular name, an object should have features similar to those of other objects with the name (e.g., sweaters tend to be soft), but more relevant here is that they also should be causally consistent with each other. Specifically, the physical features should be components of the causes of the object's function. This could explain why Malt and Johnson's participants believed that a sweater couldn't be rubber. Being rubber has the causal consequence of being waterproof, and that is not normally a function of sweaters. In the experiments by Kemler Nelson and her colleagues, children used names to refer to objects whose physical structure was understood to have the same causal consequences as other objects with the same name. In all cases, a name was deemed good to the extent that it picked out an object whose physical structure causally supports the known function.

The HIPE theory predicts that all aspects of an artifact can be important to categorizing, even historical role and agent intention. However, these aspects should have a lot of influence only in the rare case in which little is known about the object's physical structure or the agent's actions, because the theory also predicts that historical role and agent intention will be screened off whenever physical structure or the agent's actions, respectively, are known. (Screening off refers to a pattern of marginal dependence and conditional independence, described in chapter 4.) In particular, as figure 9.4 makes clear, the theory predicts that judgments of functional outcome should not be influenced by knowledge of the object's historically intended role if its physical structure is completely known or by knowledge of the agent's intention if the agent's actions are fully specified. Chaigneau, Barsalou, and Sloman report experimental results largely consistent with these predictions.

Causal Models of Natural Kinds

A similar theory could be developed for natural kinds such as living things. One possibility would be an abstract causal model of living things that looks like this.

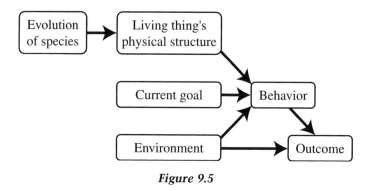

Figure 9.5

Of course, this causal model will not be shared by everyone, not by those who don't believe in evolution, for example. How to think about a living thing's current goals is also not trivial. For instance, do goals have external causes? Are goals better thought of as aspects of physical structure? You might have different intuitions about how to answer these questions for plants versus animals and even for different sorts of animals.

This causal model is abstract and approximate in other ways as well. We all know that living things participate in cycles of causation. First, outcomes of behaviors are actually causes of evolutionary change so that the causal model really cycles back on itself. However, for most purposes this can be ignored because evolution is so slow that its causal implications are negligible. Second, physical structures are themselves cyclical. Physiological systems involve complex circuits of activity. In the circulatory system, for example, the heart pumps blood around the body, including to itself. So the heart's operation depends on itself. At some level, causal models of living things are much more complicated and cyclical than the simple approximation shown here.[16] But those complications may not always be relevant to how we think about living things. Sometimes we simplify by imagining that behaviors just have one direction of influence, as shown in the diagram. We may appeal to the kind of noncircular causality embodied by the diagram to explain behaviors like why a dog is barking or why a person is yelling.

Illustrating Causal Model Theory

Whatever its domain of application, the idea of a causal model theory of conceptual structure assumes two parts to the process of categorization. First, there is some sensory experience, and, second, this sensory experience is used as a cue to retrieve conceptual knowledge from memory in the form of a causal model. The sensory experience might consist of a visual form (like an airplane shape), a sound (a roar), with some spatiotemporal context (movement in the sky). Alternatively, when one is reading, it might consist of a series of marks on a page that spell a word (e.g., a-i-r-p-l-a-n-e).

These sensory features are then projected to memory. The job of memory is to retrieve the causal model that fits those sensory features best. Which model fits best? Remember that a causal model is supposed to explain why things are the way they are. For this reason, some people refer to causal models as *generative*. The job of a causal model is to explain what generated the sensory features that have been perceived, to answer the question "what would have generated the sensory experience that actually occurred?" Therefore, the causal model retrieved from memory will be the one that answers this question best. It is the causal model that makes the perceived sensory features the most likely, given any background knowledge.[17]

I'll try to make this concrete. Part of the causal model of artifact knowledge was the link from physical structure to outcome.

Figure 9.6

Let's focus on this part of our knowledge base because much of the knowledge we have about artifacts involves specifying this relation. Most people have access to many causal models that specify this relation. Here are some simplified versions of three such models. To keep things really simple, imagine that each variable is binary; it is either present or absent. Figure 9.7 represents an airplane; figure 9.8, a bird; figure 9.9, a car.

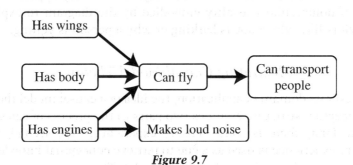

Figure 9.7

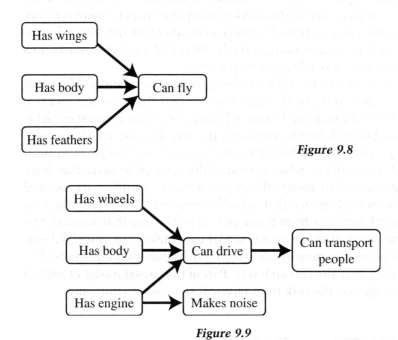

Figure 9.8

Figure 9.9

Imagine that you look up at the sky, and you perceive a moving visual form that you're able to interpret as wings and a body, and you hear a roaring sound. According to the causal model framework of categorization, you would project this sensory information to memory. (Well, wings and a body aren't really sensory; some interpretation has already gone into deriving them, but let's not get picky.) Memory's job is to find the causal model that best explains what you've sensed. If you have only the three possibilities as shown, your job is easy. The bird causal model can explain why you've encountered wings and a body and even why the object is in the sky (because it can fly). But it can't explain the loud noise. The car causal model can explain some noise, but it can't explain the wings. And in fact, it would lead you to wrongly expect wheels. The clear winner is the airplane causal model. It can explain everything you perceived, and it leads you to have further beliefs that are likely to be correct. It leads you to believe that the object is transporting people because that's an effect of airplanes.

In the real world, you would also have to compare your sensory experience with many other causal models. But the basic principle would be the same. Presumably none of them would provide a better explanation for your observations than the airplane one. If one did, then the theory would predict that that's the one you would use to categorize.

Some Implications

I pointed out earlier that, in some cases, like the raccoon/skunk example, nonobservable properties took on greater importance than observable ones. But according to the causal model framework, it's not nonobservability per se that makes a feature important; it's the fact that it plays a role in many causal relations. For some categories, causal laws tend to govern rather superficial properties that are directly observable. The chief causal relations that stop signs participate in involve such surface properties, like color, shape, and lettering. For such categories, observable features should be the most important.

The role of causal models in categorization converges with demonstrations that categories are formed in a way that depends on how they are used. For example, the category of *food* consists of a hodgepodge of grains, roots, stems, leaves, dead animals, minerals, and so on, whose only commonality is that they are consumed by living things.[18] The relevant causal model here (fig. 9.10) is simple and relevant to an important human interest, eating.

We carve up the world in different ways depending on what's on our minds. Some of those carvings are frequent enough that they become part of our language and we assign them a name, like *food*. They are frequent because the causal model they are associated with tells us about achieving an outcome that is very important to us, in this case critical to our survival.

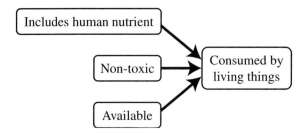

Figure 9.10

The take-home lesson from this discussion is not that every object is associated with a single causal model, because objects don't necessarily have just one causal model. A single object may have many; which one is selected depends on the perspective one is taking at the moment (categorization has as many perspectives as a Picasso painting during his Cubist period). People have different intentions when dealing with an object, and the causal model at issue will depend on the current intention. Thinking about someone in his role as a father will elicit a causal model about birth and upbringing, but thinking about the same person as an employee elicits a causal model of work and wage earning; saying he's a "poet" induces a causal model about the effects that words have on people. The take-home lesson should be instead that, whatever one's intention in a particular context, the relevant knowledge will be organized around a causal model.

Causal Versus Other Kinds of Relations

How do we know that causal knowledge—as opposed to other types of knowledge—is so important to categorization? After all, not all knowledge is causal; some of it concerns part-whole relations, class inclusion relations, and so on. A part of the answer is empirical. Studies show that people aren't always able to make as much use of noncausal forms of knowledge. Several studies have shown that attributes are treated as important in category membership judgments to the extent that they participate in causal relations. For instance, an object with all the features of a robin except that it doesn't eat is judged harder to imagine than an object with all the features of a robin except that it doesn't chirp.[19] The attribute *can eat* participates in more causal relations than the attribute *can chirp*. It's hard to imagine a robin that can't eat and yet can fly and breathe and do all the other things typical robins do because a robin that can't eat can hardly do anything (except die). But a robin that can't chirp is just a quiet robin. It's not a matter of which attributes we normally use to pick out robins because we rarely say, "Look, that thing is eating; it must be a robin!" In fact, we're more likely to say, "Look, that thing is chirping; it must be a robin!" Yet eating is more important for deciding what to call it.

In contrast to this strong evidence for the importance of causal relations in naming, there is evidence against the use of class inclusion relations. Class inclusion relations tell us that if As are Bs and Bs are Cs, then As are Cs. This is called transitivity. But name categories aren't always transitive. Most people will agree that a car seat is a seat. And most people will agree that a seat is furniture. But nobody will agree that a car seat is furniture.[20] The way people organize category knowledge does not always obey the dictates of class inclusion.

In contrast, part-whole knowledge plays a large role in structuring our knowledge of categories. For example, to know what a bicycle is, in part, is to know that it has wheels and a handlebar. But causal mechanisms tie the parts together into a whole. Bicycles have the parts that let them serve their function, the bodies of living things have parts that afford the causal powers for survival, decorative parts attract other agents, and so on. So causal knowledge is in this sense the most fundamental.

Noncausal relations are not entirely irrelevant to categorization. For instance, sometimes we'll appeal to a particularly salient property to name something. If asked to name an object quickly, perceiving a red breast may be sufficient to call it a robin because red breasts are so easy to pick out perceptually despite not having many causal roles. Sometimes we'll appeal to properties that distinguish the object we're naming from other objects in the context. If I'm trying to draw your attention to the only blue car in a parking lot full of cars, I might refer to the "blue" one even though blue is hardly causally central of cars. Categorization serves multiple purposes, and not all those purposes are served by referring to causally central properties. Causal models are most important when the purpose of categorizing is to reveal why an object exists, what it is for, where it comes from, and how it works.

Basic-level Categories and Typical Instances

Many years ago, the psychologist Roger Brown made the important point that, first, objects can be named at different levels of abstraction.[21] A robin can be referred to as a robin or, more abstractly, as a bird, or, more abstractly still, as an animal or even as a three-dimensional entity. Or it can be labelled more specifically, as a female American robin say. Second, Brown pointed out that one level "has a superior status." Here's how he said it: "While a dime can be called a coin or money or a 1952 dime, we somehow feel that *dime* is its real name. The other categorizations seem like achievements of the imagination." Brown called this level with a superior status the *basic level of categorization.*

This point recalls the discussion in chapter 4 of levels of causality. Causal models can be described at multiple levels. Abstract models are coarse descriptions of how a mechanism works. The higher you go, the more details of the causal model you ignore. Incorporating Brown's insight, we see that there must be a basic level of causal modeling, a level that normally gives us the appropriate amount of information to suit our purposes—not too much, because then we'd have to worry about details that don't provide added value, and not too little, because then we wouldn't have the information we need to decide what to call something. The level presumably changes with expertise. Experts rely on more detailed causal models, and therefore they use names at lower levels of abstraction, names that have more precision. For example, soccer enthusiasts have refined causal models of various teams and styles of play, and they have a correspondingly rich vocabulary for talking about the game. Who but a British soccer expert, for instance, would know what "selling the dummy" means? (Answer: deceiving the opposition into believing the ball is going to one player when in fact it is going to another.) This is why computer geeks are so hard to understand, because they are thinking and talking at a more detailed level of analysis about computers than anyone else is interested in.

Another important fact about categories is that not all members are equal. Some are better examples than others; some are more *typical* than others. Robins are more typical birds than ostriches, and hammers are more typical tools than vise-grips.[22] According to causal model theory, this is because our causal models do a better job of explaining some category members than others. The attributes of typical category instances fit the causal model better than the attributes of atypical category members. (Speaking formally, we'd say that the features of typical instances are more likely, given the causal model, than the features of atypical instances.) As an illustration, our causal model of birds tells us that wings and feathers are used for flying. Robins satisfy this rule in that they have wings and feathers and they fly. But ostriches violate it because they don't fly. So the causal model of birds explains robins' features better than ostriches' features.[23]

Conclusion

The application of causal model theory to conceptual structure implies that people try to explain the features of objects in terms of other object features. Categories emerge in order to describe the sets of causal relations that tend to go together (e.g., things that are round and fuzzy and smell nice will cause the desire to stroke or embrace). Causal models are an excellent way to talk about much of the general knowledge we have about objects.

The idea is that an object is judged a category member to the extent that it can participate in the causal relations that objects of that type participate in. Something is "water" if, under the right conditions, it would freeze, evaporate, quench thirst, flow through hydroelectric dams, and so on, if in general it is governed by the causal laws that govern things of that type.[24] This is not a new idea. The philosopher C. I. Lewis made the point in 1929: "Categories are what obey causal laws."[25]

10

Categorical Induction

How do we come to have beliefs about statements that we've never thought about before? Sometimes we do it through calculation or derivation. I can calculate that the square root of 361 is 19 or measure the minimum length of leather I need to make a new belt (more than I care to admit). We can think of such conclusions as *deductive*. Given a set of assumptions or premises (like the size of my waist) and some rules (like how to count, multiply, and add), we can believe the conclusion we derive with certainty. As long as we're talking about base 10 arithmetic, the square root of 361 is not a matter of belief or conjecture. I can *prove* that it's 19. Deduction can be important in everyday conversation. If someone says, "My favorite candidate is Republican and I always vote for my favorite candidate. Therefore, I voted Democratic," then you should feel free to take that person to task because their conclusion doesn't deductively follow from their premises; they're being inconsistent.

But deduction is not the bread and butter of everyday cognition. Deduction is so difficult for people that we relegate as much of it as we can to computers and to well-trained experts who apparently are able to make sense of the U.S. tax code, for example. People are able to reason in a number of ways better than they can reason deductively. We can reason by analogy, reason by example, reason vaguely, and reason causally. But now I'm getting ahead of myself.

Some beliefs we come to by direct observation, some by hearing about them. I know the Mediterranean Sea exists and that it's a most inviting blue because I've seen it. I know the Great Coral Reef exists and that it's a spectacular strange world of color and life because I've been told about it. Of course, I can only observe or hear about a finite number of things. Yet I also know that all the seas of the world are wet though I haven't seen all of them, nor has anyone told me that they're all wet. I could have deduced it, I suppose, from the premises that all the seas are full of water and that water is wet. But how do I know those things? Nobody has informed me that all the seas are full of water nor that all water is wet. In fact, I'm not absolutely certain that both these claims are true.

Many of the things I know are generalizations from particular facts. I discover a few particular examples (a few ravens that are black), and I generalize to the whole class (that all ravens are black). Although I generalize all the time, and although I feel pretty confident most of the time in my conclusions, I can never be absolutely sure. Such conclusions are inductive, and inductive conclusions can be drawn only with some probability (greater than 0 but less than 1). No matter how many times we see the sun rise in the morning, we can't know for sure that it will rise *every* morning. Our belief that the sun will rise tomorrow is to some extent guesswork.

Induction and Causal Models

In the 18th century the philosopher David Hume argued that induction is uncertain in his seminal work on how people make inductive inferences and how those inferences can be justified. Way ahead of his time, Hume argued that inductive inference depends on relations of cause and effect.[1]

We can think about the relation between causation and induction in terms of causal models. We see the sun rise every morning. But we don't jump to the conclusion that the sun will rise every morning. Instead, we try to understand why the sun is rising. The ancient Egyptians resorted to postulating that the sun spent the night traveling deep underground in order to arrive in the east so it could spend the daytime traveling west.[2] The causal models of Western civilization were dominated for at least 14 centuries by the Ptolemaic geocentric theory that the universe revolves around the earth. To explain the observed motion of the stars and planets, Ptolemy catalogued a complex system of epicycles according to which celestial objects rotated circularly on the circumference of

the circular path of other celestial objects. It was all very complicated. After hundreds of years of thought, discussion, and battle,
Western scientists finally agreed that, in fact, our solar system revolves around the sun. So a causal model of the solar system came
into being that supported many general statements about the planets
and their relative distances. One of the model's predictions is that the
sun will continue to rise every morning (at least for the next 5 billion
years or so).

So the induction, the claim that the sun will rise every morning,
does not come directly from our observations of the sun rising in
days gone by. Rather, it comes from the current causal model of
why the sun has always risen in the past, a causal model that has so
far always predicted that it will also rise tomorrow. More generally,
universal conclusions that we draw from particular facts are commonly mediated by the construction of a causal model to explain
the facts. The universal conclusion is just a description of the causal
model or (more often) some causal relation embedded in it.

Argument Strength: Similarity and Causal Knowledge

Psychologists have tended to focus on more earthly forms of induction.[3] They have studied, for example, how people induce new
properties of animals. Suppose I tell you that chickens have a liver
with two chambers and then ask you, based on that fact, which of
the following is more likely:

1. Hawks have a liver with two chambers.
2. Penguins have a liver with two chambers.

This is not exactly the same sense of induction just discussed, of
generalization from particulars to a universal. Here, we're instead
projecting a property (having a liver with two chambers) from one
basic category (chickens) to another (hawks). But the difference isn't
terribly significant. After all, you can think about the process as
generalizing from a particular (chickens) to a universal (all birds) and
then specializing the conclusion back down to a particular (hawks).
And even if you don't believe that this is the process people actually
go through to decide which statement is more likely, the task nevertheless involves a judgment about one category, given knowledge
about a different category under conditions of uncertainty. And this
is the heart of induction: how people make guesses about the world
is based on information that doesn't permit them to prove a conclusion but only to increase their degree-of-belief in the conclusion.

Given the two choices, most people will choose the first answer, hawks. Hawks are more similar to chickens than penguins are, and people generally choose the more similar category when they have nothing else to go on. Similarity is a basic principle of induction. Similarity can be overridden, however. Evan Heit and Joshua Rubinstein[4] asked people to evaluate the strength of the following two arguments:

1a. Chickens have a liver with two chambers; therefore, hawks have a liver with two chambers.
1b. Tigers have a liver with two chambers; therefore, hawks have a liver with two chambers.

Most people found 1a stronger than 1b; the inference about anatomy from chickens to hawks was stronger than the inference from tigers to hawks. This is much like the example we just saw. Chickens and hawks are more similar than tigers and hawks; therefore, it is more natural to make an inductive leap to hawks from chickens than from tigers. But now consider the following pair of arguments:

2a. Chickens prefer to feed at night; therefore, hawks prefer to feed at night.
2b. Tigers prefer to feed at night; therefore, hawks prefer to feed at night.

This time people judge the argument about tigers (2b) to be stronger than the argument about chickens (2a). When we're talking about feeding behavior, rather than anatomy, tigers and hawks seem more similar than chickens and hawks.

We can explain these results in terms of causal models. People might ask themselves, how would this property come to be for the respective animals? And would the causal process that explains the property be more similar for one pair or for the other? To be more concrete, to judge the first pair of arguments, people could have generated causal models to explain the origin of the anatomical structure of chickens, hawks, and tigers. Of course, most people know very little about the origin of anatomical structure; therefore, their models would be extremely vague and simplistic. It might not be much more detailed than the following:

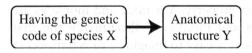

Figure 10.1

Once you have a causal model in hand, even one as vague as this, it is clear how to proceed to make the judgment. Chickens and hawks are both birds, so they surely have more similar genetic codes than tigers and hawks. A reasonable assumption is that, because anatomical structure is the effect of genetic code, anatomical structure will be similar if genetic structure is, and thus, we can expect chickens and hawks to have a more similar anatomical structure. Therefore, hawks are more likely to have a liver with two chambers if chickens do than if tigers do. When you spell it out, the chain of reasoning is a little long, but each step is natural. If causal models are at the center of how we think about the world, such reasoning could happen quickly, effectively, and automatically.

What about the other pair of arguments about feeding at night? Why do people's choices reverse? Because a different causal model is operative. Both tigers and hawks are known to be predators, and chickens are not, so our knowledge about the feeding habits of tigers and hawks includes a causal relation like the following:

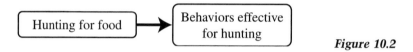

Figure 10.2

But our knowledge about chickens would not include this link. Therefore, for this property, the causal models for tigers and hawks are more similar, leading to the opposite conclusion.

Argument Strength: Causal Principles Are Sufficient

So we see that both similarity and causality are important for making inductive inferences across categories. But it is not similarity per se that is important; it is the similarity of the aspects or features of a category that are causally responsible for the property in question that mediate induction.

When the causal model is simple and clear enough that people can appeal to it directly, then there's no need to make guesses based on similarity. The argument that bananas have some property and therefore monkeys have that property is judged stronger by more people than the argument that mice have some property, and therefore monkeys have that property. Yet mice and monkeys are more similar than bananas and monkeys.[5] Presumably the first argument is stronger because it is easy to imagine a causal model in which the property is transferred from bananas to monkeys. The causal model would derive from the general causal principle shown here:

Figure 10.3

No such causal principle normally directly transfers properties from mice to monkeys (although I did once see a monkey eating a mouse in a zoo in Barcelona).

A closely related phenomenon is that induction is mediated by the way people explain facts. A fact increases belief in another fact if the two share an explanation. For example, telling people that boxers are not eligible for most health insurance plans increased their judgment of the probability that asbestos removers are not eligible either.[6] The common explanation depends on the causal relations.

Figure 10.4

However, telling people that boxers are more likely than average to develop a neurological disorder actually decreased their judged probability that asbestos removers are more likely than average to develop a neurological disorder. In this case, the causal model for boxers (having to do with getting hit in the head frequently) is different from the causal model for asbestos removers (having to do with inhaling a dangerous substance). Suggesting an explanation that doesn't match the causal model of the fact being judged leads people to discount the plausibility of the fact (perhaps related to the discounting effect discussed in chapter 9). In both cases, the willingness to believe a fact is influenced, if not governed, by the construction of a causal model in an attempt to explain how the fact could be true.

Causal Explanations

Notice how quickly and easily causal explanations come to mind in all the examples discussed. Constructing a causal explanation is not a trivial affair. It requires retrieving causal relations from a vast warehouse of facts in memory and stringing them together in a plausible way that satisfies your explanatory goal. The ease people exhibit in doing so suggests that the construction of causal models is a fundamental cognitive process.

Notice also that in all these examples, it is the principles for generating causal models that people have access to in order to make inductions and not causal models per se. Causal models aren't necessarily waiting like ripe cherries to be picked from memory; they have to be constructed for a particular purpose. The availability of abstract causal relations that can be applied to a variety of different cases is what allows us to do so.

Causal Analysis Versus Counting Instances: The Inside Versus the Outside

Say you know that one or more members of a tribe have two properties. One property is like skin color in that you know it doesn't vary too much within a tribe. The other property is like obesity; you know that it tends to vary a lot within a group of people. Which of the two properties is more likely to be shared by other members of the tribe? Presumably, the less variable property, skin color, is. This is true almost by definition. Properties that don't vary much will be more likely to hold in all category members if they are found in a couple of category members than properties that do vary. In other words, properties that don't vary are more likely to be induced than properties that do vary. Again, people tend to agree with this reasoning and act accordingly.[7]

But the fact that people's willingness to make an induction differs depending on the variability of a property does not imply that variability itself is vitally important to people. People could be making their inductions on some other basis—without thinking about variability—but variability could nevertheless influence judgment because it is correlated with something that people do care about. More specifically, people could make inductions based on causal models that do not represent variability explicitly but do represent something else that correlates with variability and thus represents variability implicitly.

One possible gauge of variability is causal centrality.[8] A property might be causally central if, for instance, it takes part in many causal relations. Skin color is more causally central than obesity because your skin color is related to your genes and thus helps identify your origin and can signify other characteristics like your susceptibility to skin cancer. Obesity is causally related to much less: how much you like to eat, how much you're able to eat, and how long you would survive without food. Similarly, in the domain of human-made artifacts, a nonobservable property of a stereo like *made with high quality audio components* is more causally central than any of its effects, like *generating high quality sound* because *high quality audio components* plays more causal roles than *generating high quality sound*. Any effects of *high quality sound* are, indirectly, also effects of *high quality audio components*. But *audio components* is causally related to events that are unrelated to *sound quality*, like cost, durability, and so forth. In each case, the more causally central property is less variable. The quality of a stereo's components shouldn't vary much among stereos of the same brand and mark because they're all made in the same way with the same materials. The components must vary less than the sound because every difference in components will have a corresponding difference in sound while the sound might vary for other reasons (bad acoustics, bad recording, etc.).

In general, properties that are causes of others must be less variable if their variation is a cause of variation in the others. So centrality is correlated with lack of variability and thus can serve as a proxy for variability; if a feature is known to be causally central, it's likely less variable than a feature known not to be central.

And the centrality of a feature is generally more available than its variability. In chapter 8, I argued that people use causal models to categorize things. If I'm right, then category labels can elicit causal models automatically. If you already have a causal model of a category, then it's easy to determine the centrality of a feature of that category. Just look to see how many links go out of it; the more links, the more central.[9] In contrast, it's not so easy to determine a property's variability. To do that, you have to think of multiple instances and count the number with the property and the number without. But the instances you think of better be representative of the whole category or your estimate will be way off. This can mean a lot of work for little gain.

You can think of a causal model as providing an *inside* view of a category. It tells you what the properties of the category are and how they relate to one another. A listing of a category's instances is an *outside* view. An outside view can be very useful for counting instances, for thinking of exceptions, and for separating instances into nonoverlapping groups. But an inside view is more useful for reasoning, making inductions and counterfactual inferences, understanding categories' propensities, and combining them (e.g., figuring out what a "muscle shirt" is requires knowing something about the causal roles of muscles and shirts).

Conclusion

Like some philosophers, some psychologists have been coming back to the view that induction is mediated by causal models,[10] causal models that are often generated online through the application of causal principles, abstract causal relations that have general applicability. Such causal models help to explain how people make inductive inferences when the inference can be conceived as a causal effect, as in the *bananas have it; therefore, monkeys have it* example.

In other cases, inference involves analogy: a predicate is applied to one category because it is known to apply to an analogous category, as in the *tigers do it; therefore, hawks do it* example. In such cases, the analogy seems to be between causal structures. Finally, causal models give a psychologically plausible way to think about why people sometimes show sensitivity to statistical information. Instead of assuming that people calculate statistics like measures of the variability of a property, the requisite information can be interpreted as a property's centrality in a causal model.

11

Locating Causal Structure in Language

We can observe people's use of causal models by listening to what they say because we talk about causal structure all the time. What is it about my team that's going to cause them to embarrass your team? Which causal model of history explains the current tension in the Middle East? What's causing Michel and Michelle's marriage to fall apart? An analysis of language also reveals that causal models underlie talk in a more subtle, deeper sense. We use causal models to produce and understand speech even when we have no idea that we're doing so. I'll focus on two aspects of language that illustrate this usage: what pronouns refer to and the meaning of conjunctions like *and* and *if*. The meaning of *if* is especially complicated, and the details of the causal model framework are particularly helpful for understanding it.

Pronouns

Consider these sentences:

1. Steven admires David because *he* is so candid.
2. Steven annoys David because *he* is so candid.

These sentences are identical in form except for their main verbs ("admires" in the first, "annoys" in the second). Yet in the first sentence, *"he"* refers to David, but in the second *"he"* refers to Steven. The reason is that in both cases *he* refers to the causal agent of the preceding verb (David is the cause of admiration, but Steven is the cause of annoyance).[1] This example shows that, whatever the machinery is in our heads that parses sentences into their parts and assigns meaning to pronouns, it is sensitive to causal structure.[2]

The influence of causal structure can get more complicated.[3] See what happens by changing the adjective in sentence 1:

> 3. Steven admires David because *he* is so naïve.

Now *he* could well refer to Steven rather than David. Naïvety seems a more likely cause of why someone should admire than why someone should be admired, and this suggests that Steven might best be viewed as the causal agent of the sentence and the pronoun should therefore refer to him. Causal analyses can be influenced by a number of considerations, which is why processes that depend on them—like choosing the reference of a pronoun—require sophisticated ways to represent and reason about causal structure.

Conjunctions

Causal structure is implicit in other uses of language. Consider the meaning of *and* in this sentence:

> Seven maids with seven mops swept the beach *and* cleared it of sand.

And here clearly implies cause: the mopping caused the clearing of sand. *And* tells us directly that two events occurred: the beach was well swept, and the beach was cleared of sand. Our causal knowledge allows us to infer that sweeping a beach for long enough will likely clear it of sand. Putting the two together, the sentence is saying that the maids swept away the sand. Of course, *and* doesn't always have a causal interpretation. Sometimes it just refers to events that happen jointly:

> The eldest oyster winked his eye *and* shook his heavy head.

Again the critical cue comes from causal knowledge. Eye winking and head shaking are causally independent, so *and* here does not suggest a causal relation. Sometimes it refers to events that happen one after the other:

> Four other oysters followed them *and* yet another four.

I imagine groups of oysters making their decisions sequentially. *And* merely connects the decisions over time. Sometimes *and* refers to events that have a kind of parallelism:

> The walrus likes oysters *and* so does the carpenter.

The carpenter likes oysters but not because the walrus does; they merely happen to share the same taste. Their preferences are causally unrelated.

But the causal meaning is a frequent one. Moreover, other conjunctions can be even more specific in the causal relation they suggest. *Because* obviously suggests a causal explanation:

> You could not see a cloud *because* no cloud was in the sky.

Even *but* can have a causal reading. For instance, it can mean that an event is causally disabling:

> The oysters would have had a fine walk along the beach *but* for the walrus's trickery.

That is, the walrus prevented the oysters from having a good time.

Various linguistic tests can be used to determine which meaning of a conjunction is intended. One test depends on the fact that pronouns generally refer to causal agents. Consider this statement:

> The walrus talked to the carpenter, and the oysters ran away from him.

This sentence has two distinct interpretations, depending on the conceptual relation between the two propositions. If we interpret it to mean that the walrus's talking caused the oysters to react, the pronoun *him* clearly refers to the walrus. But if we interpret the sentence as expressing a parallelism between the actions of the walrus and the actions of the oysters, that they both separately acted as agents, one by talking and the other by running, then the pronoun is interpreted as referring to the carpenter.

These simple examples show how deeply causal considerations penetrate everyday speech. They penetrate so deeply that we're not even aware that they're there.

If

"If" has a huge number of meanings. Consider only some of the contexts in which it is used:

- A promise: If you cover me with strawberry jam, then I'll do the same for you.
- A threat: If you cover me with strawberry jam, then I'll tar and feather you.

- A warning: If you drink from his gourd, then you'll break out with sores.
- A bargain: If you give me a hamburger today, then I will give you $5 on Tuesday.
- An observation: If there is thunder, then there is lightning.
- An instruction: If you tell that joke, then pause before the punchline.
- A fantasy: If Mont Blanc were made of whipped cream, then I would live in France.
- A rule: If you are drinking alcohol, then you must be over 21.
- A diagnostic: If she becomes world champion, then the vitamin supplements were worth the expense.
- A direct cause: If alcohol is in the blood, then judgment is impaired.

"If" or "If...then" may carry common meaning across all these contexts. Nevertheless, it is plain that the meanings are not identical.

The Material Conditional

Propositional logic is the most familiar kind of logic, the one taught in the classroom. Propositional logic treats statements like "if A then B" as meaning that three possibilities can be true:

1. A and B are both true.
2. A is false but B is true.
3. A and B are both false.

The latter two are not obvious. The idea is that if A is false, then "If A then B" must be true regardless of whether B is true or false because there's no way to disconfirm the statement. The propositional logician's intuition is that a statement like "if pigs had wings, then horses could fly" is true because pigs don't have wings, so it isn't possible to observe a counterexample to the statement (a case in which pigs have wings but horses don't fly).[4] And in the absence of a counterexample, the statement must be true! This interpretation of *if* is called the *material conditional*. It is equivalent to the statement that either A is false or B is true. That is, if either A is false or B is true, then one of the three possibilities holds, and therefore "If A then B" is true.

Of the examples, only the warning, the observation, the diagnostic, and the direct cause seem, on the face of it, to have any correspondence to the material conditional. All three are propositions, statements that can be true or false. All three would seem to be true in the three situations that define the material conditional. Consider the warning, "If you drink from his gourd, then you'll break out with sores." This is true in the event that

1. You drank from his gourd and you broke out with sores.
2. You did not drink from his gourd and you broke out with sores.
3. You did not drink from his gourd and you did not break out with sores.

It is false in the event that

4. You drank from the gourd and you did not break out with sores.

The observation "If there is thunder, then there is lightning" is true for its three corresponding possibilities:

1. There was thunder and lightning.
2. There was no thunder but there was lightning.
3. There was neither thunder nor lightning.

And false for the fourth possibility:

4. There was thunder but no lightning.

Similarly, the cause "If alcohol is in the blood, then judgment is impaired" is true only when:

1. There is alcohol in the blood and judgment is impaired.
2. There is no alcohol in the blood and judgment is impaired.
3. There is no alcohol in the blood and judgment is not impaired.

Relevance Before Truth

Yet the remaining examples of if-then statements aren't even about what's true or false! Consider the first one, the promise: If you cover me with strawberry jam, then I'll do the same for you. The right question isn't whether it's true but whether it's believable or desirable. In fact, if you don't cover me with strawberry jam, it seems to me that you'll never really find out if it's true. A logician might argue that if you don't cover me with strawberry jam, then we're in case 2 or 3 as shown in the list. Either I'll cover you with strawberry jam or I won't. In either case, the statement is true. But this seems like a word game. If I utter such a promise, then the only case that I'm really talking about is how I'll respond if I become all sticky after meeting you. The question you should ask yourself is not whether one of the three "true" possibilities would hold, but rather whether you can believe me and, if so, how much you like strawberry jam. The material conditional is just the wrong way to think about the meaning of a promise.

An analogous argument could be made about threats, bargains, instructions, fantasies, and even rules of the sort illustrated. Their relevance isn't in their truth but in their degree of credibility and in the consequences that they indicate. Even when if-then statements are about truth, like in the case of warnings and observations, the value of the statement still comes from the information imparted by the consequent (the *then* part of the statement) when the antecedent (the *if* part) holds.

Indicatives Versus Counterfactuals

The difference between different kinds of if-then statements can be quite subtle. Philosophers have discussed at length the difference between these two statements:

1. If Oswald didn't kill Kennedy, someone else did.
2. If Oswald hadn't killed Kennedy, someone else would have.

Most people agree with the first statement but hesitate with regard to the second.[5] The first sentence is apparently about what actually happened in Dallas in 1963, and we know that Kennedy was shot, so somebody must have shot him. If it wasn't Oswald, it must have been someone else. But the second assumes that Oswald shot him and then asks about another possible world, a counterfactual, in which Oswald hadn't. What would have happened then? The philosopher David Lewis uses this kind of example to distinguish between two fundamentally different kinds of if-then statements: *indicatives* and *counterfactuals*.[6]

Examples like the first sentence show something else as well. Not only is it true, but its *converse* is also true. If someone else killed Kennedy, then Oswald didn't. Sometimes we say, "if p then q," but we also mean "if q then p." We implicate the two meanings when, for example, we use *if* to strike a bargain. I'll give you $5 on Tuesday for a hamburger today, and, rest assured, I won't give you $5 on Tuesday if you don't give me a hamburger today. In other words, the bargain also implies its converse. If I give you $5 on

Tuesday, then you give me a hamburger today. Many if-then statements invite this kind of inference that gives statements a symmetric character (called a *biconditional*).

We've seen that a naïve logical interpretation of if-then statements, the material conditional, will rarely reveal what someone is trying to say when they utter a conditional. People are just not usually trying to claim that one of three possibilities is true (A and B, not A and B, or A and not B). Instead, people are usually focused on something else. Frequently, the intended meaning of *if p then q* depends only on whether q would hold if p did. What would happen if p did not occur is just irrelevant. Moreover, whether p or q or both happen to be true in the actual world just isn't the point. We would probably all agree with the statement that "if Shakespeare didn't write all those plays, then somebody else did" (perhaps somebody else named William Shakespeare?). We believe this statement even though both the antecedent (if) clause and the consequent (then) clause are unknown and probably unknowable with any certainty. The representation of whether something *would* hold is just not in the domain of propositional logic, which is concerned with whether propositions are true or false.

How Far Is the Closest Possible World?

The philosopher F. P. Ramsey suggested a different way of thinking about *if* as far back as the 1920s.[7] He suggested that to evaluate *if p then q* we think of a world in which p is true and then see how likely q is in that world. That is, evaluating *if p then q* is just like evaluating the conditional probability of q, given that p is true. Philosophers, especially Robert Stalnaker and David Lewis,[8] elaborated on Ramsey's idea by developing logical systems that say essentially that the effect of *if* in language is to have us suppose or imagine that the antecedent ("Shakespeare didn't write all those plays") is true, even if it is known to be false, in which case we must imagine some other possible world in which it is true. If we have to imagine another possible world (i.e., a counterfactual world), then they suggest we imagine the closest one in which the antecedent is true and look to see if the consequent holds in that world.

For instance, to understand *if* in the context of a threat—if you cover me with strawberry jam, then I'll tar and feather you—we must imagine the world in which you cover me with strawberry jam, something you would never do. Therefore, the world we must imagine is not the actual world but a different one. What world is it exactly? It's the closest possible one in which you cover me with strawberry jam. It's the world in which everything is the same as in this world except that you cover me with strawberry jam.

Well, not everything. If everything else were the same, then I wouldn't tar and feather you on the assumption that I won't tar and feather you in the actual world. But I will tar and feather you if you cover with me strawberry jam. So at least some of the consequences of your action must be different in this other possible world than in the real world for the threat to be serious. In other words, Stalnaker and Lewis face a problem. It's not immediately obvious how the "closest possible world" differs from the actual one. For instance, does the closest possible world contain one more empty jam jar than the actual world? When exactly is one world closer than another?

To see the crux of Stalnaker and Lewis's problem, consider this sentence: "If the United States invaded Europe, then there would be a World War III." According to possible-worlds logic, we need to consider the closest possible world in which the United States invades Europe and decide whether there would be a third world war in that world. But you might argue that there would not be a war in that world because there hasn't been (at the time of writing) a third war in this world, and we're considering the possible world that's most similar to this world. That is, the statement must be false because the possible world in which there is a a third war is much more distant (less similar) to the actual world than the world in which there is no World War III. This is a problem for Stalnaker and Lewis because, according to their logic, we don't want to decide whether q is true in another world by seeing if it's true in this world. If that's all we had to do, we wouldn't even need the other possible world; we could decide on the basis of the truth value of q in this world. Moreover, the analysis gets the truth value of the statement wrong. Is the statement really false? It may be unlikely that the United States will invade Europe, but if it does, is World War III so hard to imagine?

Causal Models Again

This is where causal models can help. Notice, first, that many if-then statements involve causal relations. Obviously, the direct cause does (If alcohol is in the blood, then judgment is impaired). The promise also lays down a causal link:

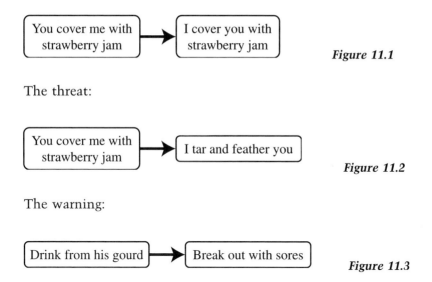

Figure 11.1

The threat:

Figure 11.2

The warning:

Figure 11.3

You get the idea.

The only if-then statements that don't state a clear causal relation are the observation, the fantasy, and the rule. However, even in these cases, there's a relevant causal model; it's just not clear what it is. In the case of "If there is thunder, then there is lightning," it could be that someone who makes such an observation believes that thunder causes lightning, that lightning causes thunder, or that something else causes both. Or the person might not know.

What's the relevant causal model for "If Mont Blanc were made of whipped cream, then I would live in France"? Presumably it has to do with how much I like whipped cream (more than is good for me). It's something like this:

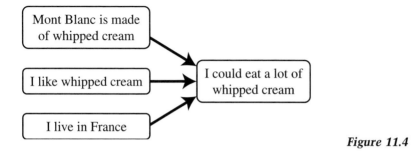

Figure 11.4

The if-then statement in this case relates two of the causes needed to produce a desired effect. The reasoning is not entirely causal. It depends on part-whole knowledge too, knowing that Mont Blanc is in France.[9]

The causal model for the rule "If you are drinking alcohol, then you must be over 21" is more complicated. This rule concerns permission. Being over 21 permits you to drink alcohol:

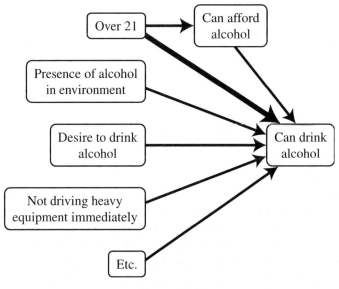

Figure 11.5

In each of these cases, a causal model is needed to understand the situation evoked by the if-then statement. This is far from the whole story in understanding the meaning of *if,* however. In each case, *if* directs attention to some part of the causal model and encourages some inference or decision. That inference or decision is not completely determined by the causal model, however; it also requires taking our interests—our intentions, obligations, and desires—into account. In this case, the effect of *if* is to cause us to build the enabling causal connection from being over 21 to being able to drink alcohol.

How Causal Models Help Solve the Closest Possible World Problem

The problem I pointed out previously is that there's a theory of how people understand if-then statements, a theory that applies when we're talking about counterfactual worlds and what to expect in such worlds. The problem was that we have to choose which counterfactual world we're talking about, which counterfactual world is most similar to the actual world?

Recall from chapter 5 the distinction between observation and action. Action was associated with the *do* operator. We use the *do* operator either to represent setting a variable by an external agent in the world or to just imagine it being set. We can ask questions like "what's the probability of some event given that we *do*(some other event)?" This is the perfect tool to use to ask about counterfactual worlds. "If Mont Blanc were made of whipped cream, then I would live in France." Because we're imagining Mont Blanc made of whipped cream, we're setting that variable all by ourselves in our own heads. This can be represented as "What's the probability that I would live in France, given that *do*(Mont Blanc is made of whipped cream)?" And the answer to this question can be gleaned from the causal model of whipped cream. The probability is higher than it is now, as we know that Mont Blanc isn't made of whipped cream, because in the world in which Mont Blanc is made of whipped cream, I make it possible to satisfy one of my desires by living in France—to eat lots of whipped cream.

Let's get back to strawberry jam. The problematic example was "If you cover me with strawberry jam, then I'll tar and feather you." The problem was that the closest possible world in which you covered me with strawberry jam was one in which I didn't tar and feather you, in direct opposition to my threat. Is there a different possible world in which I do tar and feather you? The *if* statement supposes that you cover me with strawberry jam. The supposition seems to suggest that I should engage in a counterfactual intervention. I should imagine that you cover me with strawberry jam and examine the outcome. On the *do* operator account, I should—in the safety of my imagination—*do*(you cover me with strawberry jam). Remember that one effect of the *do* operator is to cut the variable being done off from its causes, but leave the variable connected to its effects. So before the *do* operation, the causal model is this:

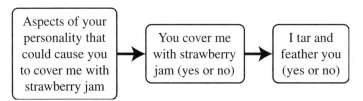

Figure 11.6

(Yes or no) appears beside the variables *You cover me* and *I tar and feather you* to mark that we don't yet know whether you do in fact cover me and whether or not I tar and feather you. Next, I imagine you covering me, represented as *do*(You cover me with strawberry jam = yes). This has the effect of (1) setting "You cover me" to yes; (2) cutting "You cover me" off from its normal causes (because it's my imagination that's setting it, not its normal causes); and (3) seeing what the effect of you covering me is. It is that I tar and feather you:

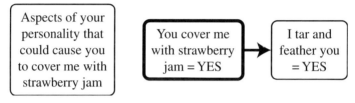

Figure 11.7

In sum, the *do* operator introduces an asymmetry. We cut the variable we're *doing* off from its causes, but not from its effects. The *do* operator thereby chooses the closest possible world for us. It's the one in which causes of our counterfactual supposition are not changed but effects are. Hence, your personality doesn't change by virtue of my imagining that you cover me with strawberry jam, but I sure do tar and feather you. This solves the problem we had choosing the closest possible world. The closest possible world seemed to be the one in which I didn't tar and feather you. But the possible world created by the *do* operation, the world obtained by doing surgery on our causal model of the actual world, is one in which I do. The general lesson is that the *do* operator applied to a causal model helps us determine the closest possible world. It's the one in which the antecedent has been cut off from its causes.

The Value of Causal Models

The meaning of counterfactual causal if-then statements is a natural domain for causal analysis because its central concern is not truth, not an assignment of propositions to values indicating their correspondence to the state of the world as logic would have us think is important.[10]

Instead, what's important is how the world works, what the mechanisms are that generate the dynamics we observe whether or not they've actually operated to construct a particular state of the world. A toaster is a causal mechanism whose causal properties can be explained even if it is off and not generating events whose descriptions have truth values. That's the nature of mechanisms. It's not whether the state they are in is true that is often most relevant; it's their ability to generate consequences, like toast (perhaps with strawberry jam).

12

Causal Learning

So far I've discussed some of the ways people use causal models in thought, language, and decision making. A burning question that I haven't yet addressed is where causal knowledge comes from. How is it acquired? Through observation? Through experiment? Is it acquired at all? Maybe causal knowledge is innate. Maybe the human genome evolved to encode the causal knowledge that was relevant to us as a species.

The idea is (slightly) less preposterous than it sounds. The psychologist John Garcia did some classic experiments on rats showing that, with no relevant prior learning, they associated illness with something they consumed (sweetened water), not with light or sound. In contrast, they associated electric shock with light or sound, not with sweetened water. Somehow rats have some innate idea about the causal propensities of water, light, and sound, knowledge they can employ without any relevant prior experience. And if rats have innate causal knowledge about types of things, people probably do too.

But not all causal knowledge is innate. It takes a long time to learn how a car works (unfortunately), never mind how to stop a video machine from flashing 12 o'clock in your living room. And even many relatively simple tasks, like opening a bottle of medication, are beyond the capabilities of small children. So the question remains, how do we acquire causal knowledge? How do we as individuals take the constant moment by moment flux of human experience and turn it into usable knowledge about the stable causal mechanisms that govern the world, mechanisms that are largely hidden from our view?

The principal answer is that we don't, not as individuals anyway. Much of our causal knowledge is furnished to us by other people. Bottles of medication say, "push down and turn," with a little arrow indicating the direction to turn. In that case, the pharmaceutical company is instructing us. Appliances come with directions for use, and software comes with a help menu. We are even taught about sex by our family or friends, or by taunts on the playground. And there's so much we don't even know. How does an electric toothbrush work anyway?

We learn much of our causal knowledge in more subtle ways from our culture. Our religious doctrines encode causal beliefs about how to remain within the law, how to benefit others, and how to achieve happiness, nirvana, or eternal salvation. Our social institutions give us lessons in how to obtain rewards from authority figures. Our language is full of causal cues. If a verb requires a subject and an object, that's a cue that it could refer to a causal action from one to the other. The language of deference ("Sir, yes sir!") enforces a power structure that has critical causal implications concerning who can force who to do what.

Another source of causal knowledge is analogy. I don't know how the circulatory system of a weasel works or whether a raven uses its claws to catch fish, but I can make a good guess by drawing analogies to more familiar animals that are similar and that live in similar environments. I've never driven an 18-wheel truck, but I bet I could get it going using my knowledge of cars. Just don't ask me to take a sharp corner or back it up.

But none of these is a sufficient explanation for causal knowledge. We all simply know too much, and much of it is never discussed, not even verbalizable. We know that we can grab objects by reaching for them or that banging metal makes a loud sound or how to make someone cry. These are examples of the huge variety of causal knowledge that we've learned directly from experience with the relevant causal system. Direct experience counts for so much because many things cannot be learned in any other way.

So how do we learn causal relations from direct experience? Theorists have a lot of ideas about this. An old school of thought in psychology called "behaviorism" studies how animals learn contingencies between stimuli and reinforcers. Some learning theorists working in this tradition believe that causal learning is just a form of associative learning and that the same principles of learning apply. Other theorists, some in psychology and others working in computer science and statistics, have developed theories of causal learning that begin with an analysis of what the best way is to learn causal relations. How would a rational learner go about acquiring causal knowledge?

A major theme of this book has been that human thought embodies the logic of intervention, that intervention in both the physical world and in imagination requires a special kind of logic, and that people are adept at using that logic. On the face of it, one would expect learning to benefit immensely from intervention, that learners should be active explorers of their environments, manipulating and experimenting, rather than being passive observers, collecting and summarizing information. Indeed, the great theorist of education John Dewey argued in the early 20th century for the benefits of active learning.

In the rest of this chapter, I will offer a selection of theories of causal learning to give the reader a sample of the ideas out there. Some of the theories come out of psychology, and some come out of rational analyses of causal learning. All tend to focus on how people use correlations, information about which events go together, to figure out what is causing what. But the world offers a number of other, supporting pieces of information about what causes what—a number of other cues to causal structure—that people are responsive to. I will mention some of these and then end with a discussion of the costs and benefits of allowing learners to actively intervene on the system they are learning.

Correlation-based Theories of Causal Strength

The most common approach to the study of causal learning is to present people with a learning problem in which event types are presorted into potential causes and effects and to investigate how the strengths of putative cause-effect links are estimated.[1] A frequent way to do this is to make up a couple of diseases (causes) and symptoms (effects). For instance, a participant might be told there are two diseases, burlotis and curtosis, and each has some symptoms, like fever, rash, and headaches. The person's task is to figure out which disease has which symptoms, that is, the strength of the relation between each cause and each effect. To make a judgment, each participant is shown some data, the disease and symptoms of several individuals. The participant might be told that Jerry has burlotis and suffers from fever and rash, while Elaine has curtosis and suffers from fever and headaches. Participants would also be shown data about Kramer and many other individuals.

From this information, participants estimate the probability of each disease and of each symptom, the probability that each symptom appears with each disease, and even the probability that each symptom appears with each other symptom. Most theories of causal learning assume that people use these numbers, a type of statistical evidence, to make their judgments of causal strength. When learning in this context, with nothing but a list of facts about individuals, the theories may be right; the participants probably do base their judgments on how often each disease matches each symptom. After all, they have little else to go on.

The theories differ in their claims about how people integrate the data. Associative theorists build on David Hume's old idea that the patterns of regularity we experience lead us to form corresponding mental associations. We build a mental association between burlotis and fever whose strength corresponds to the frequency with which we've seen them together. The process isn't this simple, though, because associations representing causal relations can't simply track the frequency of the co-occurrence of events; otherwise, we'd all think clouds cause sunshine because the two go together so often.

Rather than tracking frequency, humans and other animals track *contingency*, the degree to which one event predicts another. A common way to measure contingency is to compare the probability of an effect if the cause is present to the probability of the effect if the cause is absent by subtracting one from the other.[2] This is called ΔP (pronounced *delta* P). For example, to find out if clouds cause rain, we would calculate the following:

$$\Delta P = P(\text{rain} \mid \text{clouds}) - P(\text{rain} \mid \text{no clouds}).$$

The probability of rain when there are clouds in the sky is higher than the probability of rain when there are no clouds, so ΔP would be positive, and we would conclude clouds are a cause of rain.

One problem with ΔP is that, in some cases, we also get a positive answer if we switch the roles of clouds and rain:

$$\Delta P = P(\text{clouds} \mid \text{rain}) - P(\text{clouds} \mid \text{no rain}).$$

This is also positive because the probability of clouds is higher when it is raining than when it isn't raining. Hence, this theory fails to distinguish what is cause and what is effect in this case; it gives a positive answer to questions in both causal directions. The underlying problem with the ΔP theory is a problem for any account of causal judgment derived from how often or how strongly events are associated in the world. Conditional probabilities are essentially just measures of correlation. Therefore, because the theory is based on conditional probabilities, it can't distinguish a correlation from a causal influence; thus, it can get causality wrong, backwards in this case. In other cases, ΔP will come out positive because two variables are correlated by virtue of a common cause, despite no direct causal relation at all. For example, New York and Boston are in the same time zone; therefore, we have the following equation:

ΔP = P(noon in NY | noon in Boston) – P(noon in NY | not noon in Boston)

The answer will be greater than 0 (it equals its maximum value of 1 actually) but not because the time in Boston causes the time in New York, rather because both are caused by their geographical proximity and conventions for determining the time. In sum, ΔP is not sufficient to decide on either the existence or direction of a causal relation. Other considerations must be used.

Other associative theories are closely related to ΔP. These theories assume a learning mechanism that makes predictions. It predicts the effects that will arise from a cause and then changes associative strengths in response to the errors in its predictions. This mechanism is often called the Rescorla-Wagner rule. Theorists have proven that, under some reasonable assumptions, this rule will eventually—after many cycles of prediction and error—lead to the same strength values as ΔP.[3] These theories are attractive because they have been tested with people and with other animals and have often proven successful. They are able to account for a variety of actual behaviors.[4]

However, ΔP cannot explain everything. For example, some experiments have found that causal judgments can vary, even when ΔP is held constant, if something else, like the probability of the effect, changes. Patricia Cheng cites situations in which ΔP is clearly unsuitable. For instance, say that you want to find out if rain causes your car to get clean. But your husband just hired the child next door to clean your car every morning. Then your car is going to be clean whether it rains or not:

ΔP = P(clean car | rain) – P(clean car | no rain) = 1 – 1 = 0.

According to ΔP, rain does not clean your car, but it seems appropriate in such a case to suspend judgment about the strength of the cause rather than assign it a value of zero. As the car is already clean because the child cleaned it, we cannot know whether the rain would have cleaned it or not. The rain has no chance to demonstrate whether it's effective.

In contrast to the associative approach, Cheng has proposed a theory that she calls "power PC."[5] Her model assumes that things in the world possess stable capacities or powers. According to the power PC theory, people posit "hidden" causal powers in order to interpret information about how causes and effects go together. Whenever a proposed causal factor to be assessed is independent of other causes, causal power can be estimated via the relative frequencies of observable events. Cheng's formulation avoids some of the problems associated with ΔP. For example, when the base rate of the effect is equal to one, when your car is always clean, the value of power is undefined, in accordance with the intuition that people suspend judgment in such cases.

The evidence that power explains judgments of causal strength is mixed. Some studies have found that judgments vary closely with power, whereas others have found that when power is held constant, judgments shift with ΔP.[6] Some experiments suggest that people are sensitive to the precise nature of the judgment question. People give different responses when asked, "To what extent does the cause lead to the effect?" and "How many out of 100 cases, none of which would show the effect if the cause were absent, do you estimate would show the effect if the cause were present?" People seem to compute different measures of causal strength flexibly, according to the test question.[7] Such a conclusion suggests that no single theory of causal strength is going to prove complete.

Structure Before Strength

Even if a single theory of causal strength could explain all the data from every experiment, it would still not be a complete theory of causal learning because people know about much more than the causal strength of independent causes. Causal strength theories concern how people judge a given cause's ability to produce a given effect. But people know a lot about complex causal structure itself. The causal systems that people encounter and understand can involve many variables that combine in diverse ways. Sets of events can be joint causes of an effect, others alternative causes. Some variables might be necessary, others sufficient; some might be enabling conditions, others disabling. Think about all the complicated causal relations involved in a car or in a bureaucracy. Theories of causal strength don't explain anything about how we put any of this

together. They concern only how we determine the strength of relation between given causes and given effects.

So a key problem learners face is figuring out what causal
structure relates a whole bunch of events or variables. Causal
learners need answers to questions such as, "Is X even relevant to Y
in the context of Z?" (For example, do I still have to limit my liquor
intake even if I stop smoking?) "Does X still matter if I know Y?"
(Does it matter how much whipped cream I have if my cholesterol
is low?"). And these are real problems because the number of possible causal structures increases incredibly quickly with the number
of relevant variables. Every time an additional variable is deemed
relevant, many new causal structures become possible.

Therefore, the problem of determining the strength of a particular cause is secondary most of the time; the primary problem is
to determine the qualitative relations among variables in order to
identify the causal structure. The structure of the world needs to be
described before quantitative estimation of particular relations is
even attempted. Imagine trying to figure out the gravitational forces
between two planets in our solar system without knowing the
number of bodies in the solar system and the directions of their
mutual influences. Knowing how objects relate to one another is
preliminary to knowing the strength of any influences.

Let's start thinking about the problem of learning causal structure from the perspective of a machine. Imagine trying to build a
machine that learns about causal relations in the most efficient and
most effective way. Several algorithms for causal structure learning
by a machine have been developed in the context of Bayesian networks. These algorithms are able to infer causal structure from statistical data based on a couple of assumptions discussed in chapter 4,
the causal Markov and the stability assumptions. There are two
main approaches; they can be thought about as incremental versus
holistic learning.

Learning Causal Structure Through
Correlational Constraints

The first is known as "constraint-based" and it approaches the
problem incrementally, one link at a time.[8] It involves two steps.
First, the data are inspected, and all correlations between pairs of
variables are calculated to find out which variables vary together and
which vary separately. Partial correlations between groups of three
variables are also calculated. These reveal whether two variables are

correlated when the third one is fixed, that is, whether the first two variables are *conditionally independent* given the third one. Second, algorithms use these correlations and partial correlations to decide what the causal structure is.

I'll illustrate with a simple example from chapter 4. Imagine you have three variables, A, B, and C. First, you see which are correlated. All are. Each variable is correlated—dependent on the other two. Now you look at the partial correlations. It turns out that all are partially correlated except A and C given B. That is, A and C are conditionally independent given B, and there are no other conditional independencies. Next, you use this information to infer a causal model. Only three structures with three variables are consistent with this set of relations (ignoring the possibility of variables that we haven't noticed or can't see):

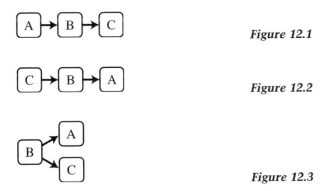

Figure 12.1

Figure 12.2

Figure 12.3

This is all the data will allow us to infer, that the correct model is one of these three. Recall from chapter 4 that these are called Markov-equivalent models because they cannot be distinguished using statistical information alone. The problem can get harder with more variables, and most causal systems do have many more than three variables. However, more variables also provide more constraints, more correlations and partial correlations that must be faithfully represented. Such constraints can reduce the number of Markov-equivalent models and help to identify a unique structure.

Is this approach to learning a plausible psychological hypothesis? What it proposes is that people encode the probabilistic dependencies in the data they experience in the form of correlations and partial correlations and use these to generate Markov-equivalent classes of causal models. Although this approach may make sense in statistical terms, there's very little evidence that this is how people actually figure out causal structure. In fact, the evidence showing that people make systematic errors in the way they judge probability and correlation (see chapter 8) makes it unlikely that people learn causal relations by first estimating correlations. This approach would be more plausible if it offered a more psychologically valid means of determining which variables are dependent and which independent.

Learning Causal Structure Through Informed Guessing

The second, Bayesian, approach to learning causal structure is more holistic. It involves taking a guess about which causal models are generating the data, based on your beliefs about the way the world works.[9] The beliefs can come from many places. They might come from the kinds of social cues discussed at the beginning of this chapter. Once you've made a guess, you can then check to see if the data are consistent with it. If they are, you strengthen your belief in the models that you guessed. If the data are inconsistent with it, you weaken your belief in the models that can't explain your observations and strengthen your belief in the models that can. Then you do it again. After multiple iterations of guessing, evaluating your guesses, and changing your beliefs accordingly, you should end up with a reasonable set of beliefs about which causal models are generating the data.

This approach should remind you of Bayesian updating, discussed in chapter 5. The idea was to use Bayes' rule to update beliefs about a hypothesis based on prior beliefs about the hypothesis's credibility, along with how well the hypothesis explained the current data. Bayesian causal learning does exactly this, with hypotheses being causal models and the measure of how well the hypothesis explains the data being the probability that the data would be generated by the hypothesized causal model.

How People Learn Causal Structure

Current data do not support a clear conclusion about whether the constraint-based view or the Bayesian view provides a more accurate account of how people learn. Nevertheless, it seems fair to say that current formulations of the Bayesian view explain more results than current formulations of the constraint-based view. However, this may reflect the great power and flexibility of Bayesianism. A theory is good only to the extent that it explains the observed data and does not provide an account of unobserved data. If it can also explain unobserved data, then it can explain anything (like an appeal to magic or to God can) and, as a result, explains nothing. The Bayesian approach may be powerful enough to explain how people learn, yet it may be so powerful that it could have provided an explanation even if people learned some other way. As Clark Glymour points out, the truth about learning causal structure may not be one or the other but some mixture of constraint-based and Bayesian-style learning.

Michael Waldmann has proposed that human causal learning should be characterized as top-down, that people impose beliefs they have about causal structure on the data that they're trying to understand.[10] This idea is consistent with the observations discussed in chapter 8 that people's judgments of probability and correlation are contaminated by their causal beliefs. Waldmann argues that people's prior knowledge and assumptions not only provide initial causal models but also shape how subsequent learning data are interpreted. To support this idea, he has shown that abstract knowledge about what's a cause and what's an effect can influence which causal structure people learn, even when the learning input—the data that people are exposed to—is held constant. Abstract knowledge about causes and effects can help people make initial guesses about causal structure and can also influence whether they believe that variables are correlated.

Insufficiency of Correlational Data

Once our focus shifts from the problem of learning how strong the relation is between a given cause and a given effect to the problem of learning causal structure among a set of variables, it becomes apparent that correlational data alone will rarely be sufficient to solve the problem; we'll need other kinds of information to select the right causal model. As we just saw, correlational data will seldom lead to a unique causal model but only to a class of Markov-equivalent models. Worse, determining causal structure with confidence from correlational data alone typically requires a lot of data per correlation to know if each correlation and partial correlation is real. Moreover, a large number of correlations are required to establish the true causal structure.

Such large amounts of data are often unavailable, and when they are, people find them hard to process. Cognitive strategies can get in the way of good data analysis. One problematic strategy is that people tend to focus on whether data support their own pet hypothesis and neglect hypotheses different from their own.[11] And cognitive resource limitations don't help either. For instance, our limited working memory span means that we can process only a small number of observations at any given time without a memory aid. And, in fact, people do struggle to learn causal structure from purely correlational data. Various studies show that no more than about 30% of adult participants can learn even simple causal structures from observation of correlational data using various procedures.

Yet, despite these difficulties, people often do learn causal structure (about cars, telephones, people, organizations, international affairs, etc.), often on the basis of a small data set, and sometimes from just a single event (think how much we learned from September 11, 2001). How do we accomplish such learning?

Cues to Causal Structure

How do people manage to acquire knowledge of causal structure, given that the correlational information supplied by our observations of the world is seldom sufficient? The answer is that they use other kinds of information. There appear to be several complimentary types:

Prior Knowledge

One reason that instruction, education, and analogy can't fully explain how people acquire causal knowledge is that they do not tell us how we, or our instructors before us, acquired the knowledge in the first place. Nevertheless, they may be able to reduce the number and complexity of causal beliefs we must discover ourselves, especially when learning about complex and culturally embedded systems.

Learning one's way through an organization—a business, a legal system, an immigration service—requires first-hand experience to know how certain people must be dealt with, to know which rules are important and which can be ignored, to know how people respond to how you dress, and so on. But your way can be made much easier by getting advice from people who have been through the system and from people who work within the organization. The set of possible causal models for you to sort through can be made much smaller with a little guidance.

Prior Assumptions

Sometimes we have hints about what pieces of the causal model should look like. Despite overall ignorance of the causal structure, we might know, for instance, that one thing is a cause and another an effect. I don't know much about cars, but I know that a causal model of how a car works should have gasoline as a cause and acceleration as an effect. Similarly, I know next to nothing about how tennis rackets are fabricated, but however it is done, the presence of raw materials must be a root cause and the finished tennis racket must be the final effect.

Some prior assumptions concern the temporal delays expected between cause and effect. Events on a pool table happen on an entirely different time scale than geological events, and we are bound to look for effects of the two types at different points in time after potential causes have occurred. York Hagmayer and Michael Waldmann have shown that the assumptions that people make about the temporal delays between events determine which events they pair together as cause and effect and also what they select as a possible cause.[12] For example, if you are trying a new drug to relieve pain and you expect the relief to come within 10 minutes, then if you experience relief an hour later you will conclude that the drug is ineffective. But if your expectation was that relief would take around an hour, you would come to the opposite conclusion.

Direct Perception of Causal Structure

In chapter 8, I discussed Michotte's studies showing that sometimes we perceive a causal relation directly. Michotte worked out in detail the conditions that lead people to see one moving object on a screen cause another to launch. For example, they must make contact; there must be no delay in launching after contact with a solid object, and so on. Michotte's work suggests that certain kinds of physical causality are directly inferred by our perceptual mechanisms. Nowadays there's evidence that even infants distinguish causal from noncausal events.[13]

In fact, our perceptual mechanisms are very sophisticated in their ability to see causality. In particular, we have a habit of inferring the initial cause of an action, the intention to behave in some way, even when the actor is merely a geometric figure moving around a screen. In work published in 1944, Fritz Heider and Mary-Ann Simmel showed people a simple film animation involving three geometric figures that moved around.[14] Observers were asked what they saw. Most people offered elaborate stories about how two of the figures were in love, how the third big bad one tried to steal away one of them, about the ensuing fight. People often even provided a Hollywood ending in which the lovers lived happily ever after. This is a lot of causal interpretation—in the form of attribution of intention—from a few seconds of a circle and some triangles moving around a screen!

Order of Information Receipt as Cue to Causal Order

The temporal order of events in experience is a highly reliable cue for causal structure in the world because effects never precede causes. This is true on a large time scale. The destruction of war is witnessed only after the speeches rallying the population to war. It is also true on an immediate time scale. The ball flies only after it is hit. Sometimes causes and effects appear to be simultaneous. Shadows appear pretty quickly after a light source shines. In general, earlier events cannot be effects of later events. Therefore, the order in which events occur is often not a bad first pass for guessing causal order. More specifically, if you perceive an event, a good first guess is that any subsequent changes in the environment are either effects of that cause or effects of an earlier common cause of that event.[15]

Such a heuristic is extremely useful but can also be misleading. For example, it can cause you to erroneously infer that you have caused an event just because it occurs immediately after you perform an unconnected action (e.g., your friend calls just as you're thinking about him, or the girl agrees to a date just after you put on your polyester suit). An athlete's superstitious behavior can also be a result of a random series of events. The baseball player who hits a home run after spitting to his right three times is liable to continue spitting to his right three times before going to bat, no matter how hard his mother tries to dissuade him. Repeated trials, however, can, in principle, identify the spurious nature of such associations to the open-minded.

People tend to be extremely sensitive to the order in which things happen over time when learning causal structure. Dave Lagnado and I have shown this sensitivity by constructing a situation in which the temporal order of events is not a cue to causal structure. We showed people three sliders that could move up and down on a computer screen. People were told that the sliders represented the state of components that were causally connected to each other. But the components didn't always relay their state to the sliders in a timely fashion. So the time at which sliders moved did not indicate how the components were causally connected. Only their correlations and partial correlations—whether the sliders moved together or not—revealed the causal relations among the underlying components. In other words, we asked the participants to ignore the temporal relations among the sliders.

What we found is that they couldn't. In some cases, we showed them the sliders moving in an order consistent with the true causal model. For example, if the model was

Figure 12.4

they would see slider X move, followed by slider Y, followed by slider Z. In the remaining cases, temporal order was inconsistent; they would see the sliders moving in the opposite order: first slider Z, then Y, then X. When asked what causal model was controlling the components, they often responded in terms of the order of the sliders' change rather than their pattern of correlations. They just couldn't ignore the temporal information.

There are certainly situations in which people do ignore temporal information. There are situations when we learn about an effect before we learn about its cause. This is the case whenever we use effects to diagnose causes, as doctors use symptoms to diagnose diseases and scientists use data to diagnose theories. But it's hard to ignore temporal information when we're watching a causal system in action.

The Interventional Advantage

What about intervention? What about the role of human action in learning? None of the discussion of theories and cues so far has acknowledged any special role for people being able to manipulate the environment that they're learning about. A role has been acknowledged elsewhere of course, by great educators like John Dewey, for example. The behaviorists even made a distinction between types of learning that roughly corresponds to the distinction between learning by intervention and learning by observation.

The behaviorists distinguished two kinds of associative learning: operant conditioning and classical conditioning. In operant

conditioning, there is a contingency between the organism's response and reinforcement; an animal is rewarded or punished for
actions it performs. Operant conditioning can be interpreted as reinforcement for interventions. The animal learns which actions
cause which rewards. Classical conditioning was made famous by
Pavlov's dogs. It involves the presentation of the reinforcer with no
contingency between response and reinforcement. Pavlov presented
dogs with food and measured how much the dogs drooled. Next, he
rang a bell before giving the food. Soon, the dogs were salivating just
from hearing the sound of the bell. They learned to expect food when
they heard the bell. In classical conditioning, the animal learns
which stimuli lead to other stimuli by just observing what follows what.

Various experiments have demonstrated that causal structure
learning is easier when people are allowed to intervene rather than
being allowed only to observe. In some situations, it's impossible to
learn merely from observation because observations don't carry
enough information to uniquely identify a causal structure. In such
cases, interventions can help. Consider an experiment by Laura
Schulz.[16] She presented 4-year-olds with two creatures: A and B.
The children were told that one of the two creatures was the boss
and that the boss made the other creature move but not vice versa
(the other creature didn't make the boss move). But the children
weren't told which creature was the boss. They had to figure out
whether the boss was A or B. No amount of observation of A's and
B's movements could reveal who was the boss because A and B were
always moving together simultaneously so there were no temporal
cues to help. In terms of causal structure, no amount of observation
could distinguish

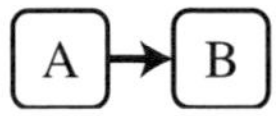

A ► B

Figure 12.5

from

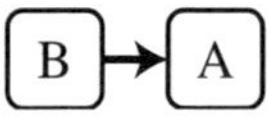

B ► A

Figure 12.6

The kids were then shown a way to intervene on the situation.
They were shown a button that made one of the creatures (B) move.
After an intervention—pressing the button—they discovered that

only creature B moved. Observing this intervention was sufficient to convince the kids (and adults too) that creature A was the boss.

Other experiments have shown that intervention helps learning using other sorts of causal structures with more variables and with different kinds of scenarios and interventions.[17] Intervention helps even if people are given a long time to learn in a situation in which it is possible to learn the causal structure from mere observation.

The Benefits of Intervention

Why does intervention facilitate learning in these experiments? Intervention offers a number of advantages. For one, as just pointed out, experimentation allows the generation of data that can discriminate between causal structures impossible to distinguish by observation alone. In Schulz's study, observation of a correlation between two variables A and B was insufficient to determine whether A causes B, or B causes A, or some third variable is a common cause of both. But interventions on B did discriminate. If the child pressed the button to move B and the result was that A then moved, then the child could infer that B causes A. If A did not move, then the child could infer that B does not cause A, either because A causes B or because they are both caused by an unspecified common cause. In principle, this could, in turn, be decided by varying A. In the same way, a child who sporadically shakes a rattle can infer that it is their action that produces the associated sound. As Pearl puts it, "The whimsical nature of free manipulation replaces the statistical notion of randomized experimentation and serves to filter sounds produced by the child's actions from those produced by the uncontrolled environmental factors."

Another advantage is that interveners can engage in systematic testing, whereas observers have no control over what they see. If you want to test whether X causes Y, then as an intervener, you can manipulate X and look for effects on Y. As an observer, you're stuck waiting for X to happen and then looking to see if Y follows. This ability to test systematically is especially helpful if you already have some idea what's going on. For instance, if you're troubleshooting a problem with your car, trying to figure out what's broken, then you can save a lot of time and trouble if you have a hypothesis (like "it's that darn starter motor again") and can then go out and test it.

The requirement on interveners to decide what intervention to make can enhance learning by focusing attention. By attending selectively to the variable that you're manipulating, it is easier to notice its direct effects than if you're trying to attend to everything that's going on. Imagine trying to figure out how an old-fashioned clock works by observing its gears and other moving parts. It will be difficult and perhaps impossible to figure out all the complex interconnections through mere observation. But if you can intervene in the system by moving gears yourself, then your attention will be drawn to the effects of your intervention. The gears that are direct effects of the gear you move will pop out. Interventions will help pick out the causal relations one by one by marking what's relevant, that is, by drawing your attention to the effects of intervened-on causes.

The Costs of Intervention

The ability to intervene does not always improve the learning situation. Intervention can also increase the difficulty of learning. One problem caused by intervention is that it can limit learning to the effects of the variables that are intervened on. When learning from observation, one can (at least in principle) learn something about the relations among all variables simultaneously. The fact that intervention focuses attention on the variables being manipulated means that variables not manipulated are less likely to be attended to. This result can hinder learning if those other variables are important causes.

This kind of problem emerges often in science. Scientists run experiments to test their pet theories. This is fine if their theories are right. But if their theories are wrong, these experiments can lead the scientists down the wrong path, causing them to test variables not all that central to the phenomena of interest. If I had more space, I'd share with you some of the lovely garden paths I've followed.

Another problem with intervention is that it changes the causal model under investigation. As we've seen in discussions of the *do* operator, an intervention disconnects the intervened-on variable from its causes. This means that you can't learn about the causes of the variable you're intervening on. More generally, it means that the learner is dealing with a different causal model for each variable intervened on. If I'm trying to understand why somebody is depressed, I will learn nothing by giving them a drug that prevents their symptoms. By masking the symptoms, I've made it impossible to use them to diagnose the causes of the individual's psychological and physical state. Only interventions on the cause of the depression, rather than on its effects, will be useful in such a case.

The final cost of intervention is that, if a variable value is set through an intervention, then that variable's normal probability of occurrence is hidden from view. If everybody is taking antidepressants, and they're effective, then it's hard to know the real incidence of depression. Maybe it's not bad to use antidepressants to solve a serious social problem if we assume the drugs have no serious consequences. But if the social problem has other causes, then perhaps it would be better to address those causes to prevent other harmful effects. But we can't do that if we intervene and thus mask the initial effect.

Conclusion

This chapter has mentioned a number of claims about how people learn about causal systems. The most that I think we can safely conclude at this point is that top-down learning is key; people make initial guesses about what is causally related to what before they ever see a system in operation, and these guesses affect their interpretation of what they see. There's still a lot to be learned about how top-down learning actually takes place. Lots of evidence points to various cues that allow people to make educated initial guesses about causal structure. But which cues get used and when they get used is still a wide open question. So is the question of how exactly new data are integrated with those initial guesses.

It's important to keep in mind how much individuals differ from one another. Some people are better learners than others, and people differ in how good they are at learning different kinds of things. Some people learn mechanical systems better than social systems and vice versa. At this point, there's no reason to believe that there's only one basic kind of causal learning that serves as a core learning process in all domains of learning. The fact that causal knowledge is expressible using causal models, a format common to many domains, seems to suggest that, at some level, there must be some common learning process. Perhaps people all learn the same way but differ in the richness of their knowledge bases. Mechanical types have access to lots of knowledge about physical mechanisms that they can use to jumpstart their learning in that domain; those with more social prowess have more, and more effectively structured, social knowledge to use. We just don't know to what extent and in what ways the tools and procedures we use to learn causal systems differ from one domain to another. We do know, however, that individuals do differ in their causal learning strategies.[18]

One question about causal learning that I have not even addressed is absolutely critical. How do people decide which variables are relevant in the first place? Most research on causal learning, and all the research reviewed in this chapter, assumes that we know which variables are relevant and that the problem is just to figure out how variables are related to one another. But we don't always know which variables are relevant; the world can be analyzed in many ways. No one set of variables necessarily has priority over others. When thinking about motion, we can say that the critical variables might be time, distance, and direction, or they might be time and velocity. Sure, one set of variables can be calculated from the other, but the choice of set to reason with can make a big difference to the process of reasoning. And, of course, different people might use different sets, and the same person might use different sets at different times to achieve different goals. Moreover, the relevant psychological variables might not have any nice correspondence to the physical variables. Maybe we think about motion only in qualitative terms (moving left, moving slowly, etc.).

The question about what the right variables are becomes huge and obvious when we think about complex systems like human behavior. How do we even begin to reduce behavior to a set of underlying parts and properties that bear causal relations to one another?

A frequent assumption is that people first choose the variables to represent a causal system and then figure out the causal structure relating the chosen variables. The idea is that people first figure out which properties or dimensions in the world matter to them and then figure out how those properties or dimensions causally relate. For instance, to learn the causal relation

Figure 12.7

one might assume that our ancestors knew the relevant variables, what it means to be hungry and what food is; their only problem was to figure out the relation between the variables, that eating food satiated their hunger.

But this assumption can't be right. How did they know what food was? Food is quite a complicated category, and it's not at all obvious what is food and what isn't (my new puppy seems to think everything is food). The variables that we reason about, like food, are actually categories of cause or effect that themselves need to be learned along with the causal structure that relates them.

Yunn-Wen Lien and Patricia Cheng offer an idea about how we do this.[19] They suggest that we learn causal categories and the structure that relates them simultaneously. Specifically, they suggest that the variables people use to represent causal structure are the variables that have the most causal power. The category "food" emerges as people discover what it is that satiates their hunger; "food" is the set of things that satisfies the causal relation shown in the figure. As a result of learning what serves this causal role, we form a new category (food). So the idea is that, instead of knowing the variables or categories and then learning how they relate causally, we use causal relations to help us figure out the variables or categories. In other words, instead of selecting variables prior to determining causal structure, people may figure out the best variables and the best causal structures together. We still need to know something about the variables to begin the process, though; we can't even get started if the slate is completely blank. So maybe some knowledge is innate after all.

13

Conclusion: Causation in the Mind

Assessing the Causal Model Framework

In the final analysis, what is the role of causal models in how the mind works? One possibility is that causal models serve as the basic language of thought from which all mental phenomena arise. On this view, causal graphs would serve as the fundamental representations that all thought operates on, both conscious and unconscious thought. All human reasoning and decision making at the deepest level would be matters of inferring effects and diagnosing causes.

But these statements are clearly much too strong. The mind engages in too many other, noncausal processes for any of these claims to be true. We can do arithmetic and geometry. Knowledge of spatial relations like which is farther west, Reno, Nevada, or Los Angeles, California, is not causal (answer: Reno). Much of the grammatical structure of language has nothing to do with causality. Simply put, the mind does much that doesn't depend on causal analysis.

But the ability to do causal analysis is nevertheless central to what it means to be human. I hope that part II of this book has convinced you that causal inference is critical in the major domains of human cognition: reasoning, decision making, judgment, language use, categorization, and learning. We see the importance of causality when we look at just about any domain that human thought is applied to. Causal models in one form or another are central in science and engineering. In chapter 8, I pointed out that legal judgment requires causal understanding. Issues of fault, blame, and guilt all depend on analyses of people's causal roles in events. Presumably an individual isn't at fault, shouldn't be blamed, and isn't guilty if they had no causal control over events. More generally, many issues of permission and obligation (issues of *deontics*) depend on causal analysis. For example, in a just world, people wouldn't be obliged to do things that they are causally incapable of doing. Clearly much more could be said about this,[1] but my point here is merely that causal models are pervasive in human thought.

So causal models in some form are central, but do those models take the form described in chapters 4 and 5? That is, is the graphical causal model formalism based on Bayesian networks psychologically plausible? The fact that not all thought is causal implies that the causal modeling framework does not serve as the basic language of thought. Moreover, the framework is hardly complete. For example, using it to make inferences about continuous processes (e.g., continuous motion) can be difficult. It also doesn't (yet) deal well with causal systems that involve cycles of causation (where one thing causes another that affects the first thing, as pedaling a bicycle causes the wheels to turn, which affects pedaling).[2] These can be real issues. For instance, decisions are often made in the context of cyclic economic systems (one simple economic cycle is that supply affects demand, which in turn affects supply, etc.).

There are no end of questions still to be answered within the causal model framework. To take only one: who we blame for a crime or accident may depend on a causal model, but how? Where must a person's action be in a causal model in order to say that person is at fault? At the beginning of the critical chain of events? Near the end? Does it depend on what other causal chains exist? There's much work to do to answer these questions and plenty of others.

Nevertheless, the causal model framework is a promising language for representing causal structure. It provides a way to represent any kind of cause—a direct cause, an enabler, a disabler, a prevention, an indirect cause, and so on. Furthermore, it allows causes to combine in any way to produce effects. In conjunctive causation, an effect requires all causes (e.g., snow melt requires both the presence of snow and the presence of enough heat to cause melting). In disjunctive causation, an effect can be produced by any one of several causes individually (e.g., heat can be produced directly by the sun or by warm air flowing in from elsewhere). Linear causation involves causes adding up to determine the size of an effect (e.g., the amount of snow melt and the amount of rain add up to determine the water level of a reservoir). Causes can combine in an indefinite number of other possible ways as well. The causal modeling framework also allows complex causal structures, like chains of causation, causal trees, and so forth.

Some limitations of the causal model framework may turn out not to be limitations at all when it comes to the framework's ability to model human thought. For instance, cycles of causation are not easy to model in the framework, but cycles of causation may not be easy for people to think about, either. Electricity is hard for many people to think about, probably because it involves cycles in the form of circuits.

The depth and value of the causal modeling framework come from its overall coherence; it is constituted by a set of plausible general principles. The framework puts together the principles spelled out in chapters 4 and 5 like screening off, Markov equivalence, explanation discounting, undoing by virtue of intervention, probability, and stability, all principles of causal reasoning that are completely general in that they apply everywhere, not just to one or another domain like animals or artifacts, but to all causal reasoning. And the framework doesn't put the principles together in some haphazard form but rather provides a coherent formal apparatus that uses sophisticated mathematical tools like probability theory, graph theory, and structural equations.

It's tempting to think of the causal modeling framework as describing a module of thought, a specialized mental tool for helping people to reason about causal processes and only about causal processes.[3] Indeed, the causal modeling framework is specialized for thinking, reasoning, and learning about a specific aspect of human experience: causal events. It assumes that cognition includes specialized representations and procedures for reasoning about causality, representations and procedures distinct from those that apply to noncausal knowledge. But conceiving of causal models as modular fails to recognize how general purpose they are, that they participate in cognition right through the processing stream, from perception through reasoning, decision making, and language.

The key idea of the causal modeling framework is that reasoning is pragmatic; it's all about helping people to achieve their goals. I believe that this is the deepest and most novel contribution of the framework to cognitive science. Because causal models are all about how actions achieve effects, at the heart of the framework is the idea that cognition is for action.

Cognition Is for Action

Let's review the fundamental claims of the causal modeling framework:

1. People, like all animals, search for invariance in order to perceive, interpret, understand, predict, and control their environments. In other words, we search for the aspects or variables in the world that reliably signal information (as a fast approaching object signals ensuing collision) useful for achieving our goals.
2. In the context of events that unfold over time, the invariants are the principles that govern the mechanisms that take causes as inputs and produce effects as outputs. The most valuable information you can have to achieve your goals is knowledge about the mechanisms that produce change. This is what causal models represent.
3. Causal models are governed by a unique logic, the logic of intervention. They provide a means, through the *do* operation, to represent and make valid inferences about the effects of physically intervening or just imagining a counterfactual intervention in a causal system. Prediction and control come from knowing what to manipulate to achieve an effect and how to perform the manipulation.
4. Human thought about causality is consistent with the logic of intervention. In simple situations, people make valid inferences about the effects of actual or counterfactual intervention with relative ease, quickly and automatically. In that sense, human thought should be understood as continuous with human action.

This seems like a sensible way to design a cognitive system. The most obvious function of cognition is to support action, so why not design the cognitive system using the very same principles and processes needed for action? Cognition on this view is an extension of our ability to act effectively, to bring about desired changes in the world.

It also seems reasonable that the mind would have evolved to serve this function. After all, all organisms act. The effect of evolutionary pressure is to select organisms whose actions are most effective in the quest for survival and reproduction. Organisms that have minds that support action in a way that permits flexibility and sophisticated reasoning should therefore have a selective advantage.

The facts about how the mind works provide additional support for these claims. The second part of the book reviewed a wide range of such facts. I reviewed evidence that all kinds of human judgment—judgments of guilt, of blame, of probability and correlation—are mediated by causal knowledge and by the ease of constructing counterfactual alternatives. People appeal frequently and automatically to causal structure to produce and comprehend English pronouns and conjunctions. The labels we choose for objects and other acts of classification appeal to the objects' causal roles. People induce new properties of categories from knowledge about other categories in large part by appealing to causal models. Even our interpretations of mathematical equations are often structured by an underlying causal model. In sum, people are highly responsive to causal structure.

The evidence that human reasoning is consistent with the logic of intervention is also strong. I've shown how human reasoning about interventions on effects conforms better to the logic of intervention than to formal logic or to probability theory. The best evidence comes from how people make decisions. Decision making turns out to make a lot more sense when choice—the act of selecting an option from an offered set—is understood as a type of intervention. Finally, people seem to be able to use interventions in order to learn causal structure. Even young children can.

Causal reasoning can even lead our reasoning astray. When we impose causal structure on noncausal relations, then we can make systematic errors in our reasoning. To illustrate, we saw in chapter 8 how causes can seem more predictive of effects than effects are of their causes, even when each is equally predictive of the other.

All in all, this book has reviewed a lot of evidence for the causal modeling framework's four claims about cognition. By no means, though, have I reported all the evidence available. A huge variety of data and theory about causal reasoning exists that I have not even mentioned. Indeed, my coverage has been quite narrow. My arguments about the centrality of causal structure and intervention in processes of reasoning and learning would have been even stronger (and more long-winded) if they had been more complete.

What Causal Models Can Contribute to Human Welfare

Why should we care about causal models? What do they offer us? The first answer is the one that this book has largely focused on, the purely intellectual answer that causal models help us to explain and understand so much both about how causal systems work in the world and about how people understand them.

On a less highfalutin plane, causal models are practical tools used increasingly often to understand complex causal systems. Applications of the technology underlying the causal model framework, Bayesian networks, and other graphical models are already in fairly wide use. They are useful for troubleshooting problems in causal systems, like figuring out why a car won't start. Computational neuroscientists are using graphical models to analyze multicellular recordings from monkey cortex. Computer scientists are using Bayes's nets to do scene recognition, to recognize spam e-mails, to build expert systems—computer applications designed to act like expert advisers—and in a host of other applications.

The greatest use of causal models currently is in the health sciences, epidemiology in particular, where they are being used to trace and predict the course of diseases as they spread through a community, diseases like cancer, infectious diseases like HIV, and others. Causal models not only provide health scientists with a lot of flexibility so that they can consider many different potential causes simultaneously but also afford the ability to ask important counterfactual questions such as, "How many patients would have died if the drug had been administered to all the people who did not receive the drug and who did die?" Because such questions involve imaginary intervention, they can be answered only using the *do* operation or its equivalent.

The ability to answer questions like this without actually administering the drug is indispensable because the drug might be dangerous or expensive. When manipulations are risky or consume substantial resources, the ability to perform the manipulation hypothetically can be invaluable. One promise of causal models, therefore, is that they will help save lives, as well as time and money.

The Human Mechanism

Cognitive scientists love to do science by metaphor, and the latest technology often provides the most captivating metaphor. Cognitive science emerged in synchrony with the development of the computer because the computer metaphor of mind was so compelling. And the metaphor created a mountain of promising new ideas. Great new insights into how people think, remember, solve problems, and make decisions came in part from thinking about the mind as a computer.

In the 1980s, new methods for computing were developed that used many relatively simple processing units all hooked up together so that computation was distributed over an entire complex network of interconnections. Such networks were sometimes called parallel distributed computing machines and sometimes called connectionist machines. Today, these kinds of networks are most frequently referred to as neural nets because the neural machinery in the brain also uses a vast number of relatively stupid processors (neurons) that are all highly interconnected. These networks laid the foundation for a new metaphor in cognitive science, what the great cognitive scientist David Rumelhart liked to call the *brain* metaphor of mind.

Causal models also derive their inspiration from a new technology, from developments in statistics and computer science for representing the structure in data and for inferring the processes that generate data. This technology has also benefited cognitive science immensely. The existence of a coherent and powerful theoretical framework to do causal analysis gives cognitive scientists a foothold in representing causal structure.

But we must be careful not to put the cart before the horse. The fact that a mathematical framework exists does not itself make it a viable description of human cognition and behavior. The jury is still out on whether the details of the causal modeling framework will provide a good description of how people actually think. The evidence that I've reviewed suggests that causal considerations and intervention are critical for understanding human thought. But whether a detailed understanding of the specific thought processes of people will come out of this project remains unknown.

The causal modeling metaphor does differ in one substantial way from the other metaphors that have appealed to cognitive scientists. Computing machinery can exist and can compute independently of human minds. They are like trees in the forest in that respect; once created, they could exist and function with no one around. But causality is more like the sound of a tree falling. Is there a sound if no one perceives it? Is there causality without someone to represent the causal relation?

I think the answer is both "yes" and "no." The "yes" answer is obvious. In the case of causality, there is a set of actual events in the world that occur over time. The "no" answer derives from the fact that what makes the relation causal includes counterfactual considerations, events that did not happen. Only an agent representing the causal relation can be aware of such nonevents. So causal models are more than just a tool for doing statistics. They are a tool whose interpretation and usefulness depends on the existence of a representing agent with the power to intervene.

Notes

1. Agency and the Role of Causation in Mental Life

1. Turing (1950).

2. For early developments in the framework, see Spirtes, Glymour, and Scheines (1993). The most comprehensive and lucid review is Pearl (2000).

3. Pearl (1988) and Pearl (2000) are already both classics. See also Halpern (2003).

2. The Information Is in the Invariants

1. Hoyle (1957).

2. Luria (1968).

3. For an interesting effort to turn chicken-sexing novices into experts, see Biederman and Shiffrar (1987).

4. Gibson (1979).

5. Russell (1913). See chapter 6.

3. What Is a Cause?

1. A rich, sophisticated, and subtle literature on causation and the relation between causes and events exists in philosophy and can be traced back to Aristotle (and maybe before). A review of that literature is well beyond the scope of this book. A solid recent review is in Woodward (2003).

2. *Works* (vol. VIII).

3. Rigorous theories of causation based on counterfactuals are offered by Halpern and Pearl (2001), Hitchcock (2001), Pearl (2000), and Woodward (2003). For a psychological analysis, see Mandel (2003).

4. See Lewis (1973) and Stalnaker (1968).

5. Hume (1748).

6. Based on Halpern and Pearl (2001).

7. Mackie (1980).

8. Halpern and Pearl (2001), Hitchcock (2001), and Woodward (2003).

4. Causal Models

1. Arnheim (1969) is a classic psychological analysis of representation.

2. This understanding of probability is often called "Bayesian" and will be briefly discussed in chapter 5. It is the perspective on probability that will be assumed in this book.

3. Assuming stability, discussed in the next section.

5. Observation Versus Action

1. Two excellent introductions to the foundations of probability are Gillies (2001) and Hacking (2001). A third conception of probability intended to unify the subjective and frequentist approaches is presented in Shafer (1996). Shafer's book also offers a conception of probabilistic causality distinct from the interventionist view I focus on later in this chapter.

2. Diagnostic inferences from symptoms to diseases and inferences from data to hypotheses are different in important ways. The former are inferences from effect (symptom) to cause (disease). Inference from data to hypothesis involves a different kind of evidential relation. The conditional probabilities connecting cause and effect are derived from causal mechanisms; those from data to hypothesis are not necessarily. Bayes' rule itself is agnostic about the interpretation of the conditional probabilities.

3. Pearl (2000), following Spirtes et al. (1993).

4. Some caveats (thanks to Clark Glymour): (1) In some cases, an intervention on a variable imposes a new probability distribution rather than setting a determinate value. (2) For cyclic graphs, the *do* operator isn't always appropriate. In general, the requirement of graph surgery is sufficient but not necessary for an event to count as an intervention. Some kinds of intervention do not entail graph surgery.

5. Keil (2003).

6. Reasoning About Causation

1. A more general framework for representing objects and events can be found in Gentner and Stevens's (1983) book *Mental Models*. Although

the chapters in that book go beyond causal reasoning, the general approach is consistent with the importance of causal structure in human reasoning.

2. Russell (1913), p. 1.

3. Russell (1948).

4. E.g., DiSessa (1993); Hunt and Minstrell (1994); Reif and Allen (1992).

5. For evidence see, for example, Andersson (1986); Driver, Guesne, and Tiberghien (1993); Reiner, Slotta, Chi, and Resnick (2000).

6. Larkin (1983).

7. Cf. Sherin (2001).

8. The essentials of this idea can be found in Forbus (1984). It's explicit in the epilogue of Pearl (2000).

9. Mochon and Sloman (2004).

10. Reviewed in Morris and Larrick (1995).

11. The idea that discounting should not occur with correlated causes is in Morris and Larrick (1995), though without the causal model motivation.

12. This study is reported in Sloman and Lagnado (2005a).

13. Sloman and Lagnado (2005a).

14. Sloman and Lagnado (2005a).

15. See Forbus (1996) for an introduction and review of this area.

16. Gentner and Stevens (1983) report early evidence.

17. For example, there's good evidence that people reason in terms of possibilities when reasoning about spatial relations, Aristotelian syllogisms, and other argument forms that tend to be construed extensionally (see Johnson-Laird & Byrne, 1991, for a review).

7. Decision Making via Causal Consequences

1. I thank Clark Glymour for this example. Much of the inspiration for this chapter came from a discussion by Meek and Glymour (1994).

2. Good, accessible discussions of rationality include Harman (1995) and Stich (1990).

3. For an empirical evaluation of expected utility as a descriptive theory, see Camerer (1995).

4. A point made by, for example, Shafer (1996).

5. Bartlett (1932).

6. Pennington and Hastie (1993).

7. See Ross and Anderson (1982).

8. Nozick (1969).

9. Another set of formal tools for describing and reasoning about decision problems that treats choice as a form of intervention is influence diagrams (Howard & Matheson, 1981).

10. See Nozick (1995).

11. Quattrone and Tversky (1984).
12. See Quattrone and Tversky (1988).

8. The Psychology of Judgment

1. Fischhoff, Slovic, and Lichtenstein (1978). For converging results showing that people tend to focus on only a single causal model, see Dougherty, Gettys, and Thomas (1997).
2. This example was inspired by Tversky and Kahneman (1980), a rich discussion of the role of causal schema in judgment.
3. Kahneman and Frederick (2002) argue that many judgment biases are a result of substituting an easy question (e.g., a question about similarity) for a difficult question (e.g., a question about probability).
4. See Tversky and Kahneman (1983).
5. Kahneman and Tversky (1982).
6. E.g., Anderson, Lepper, and Ross (1980). A comprehensive review is in Ross and Anderson (1982).
7. Michotte (1946).
8. Chapman and Chapman (1969).
9. Gilovich, Vallone, and Tversky (1985).
10. Keren and Wagenaar (1985).
11. Ajzen (1977).
12. Wells (1992).

9. Causality and Conceptual Structure

1. Bruner (1973).
2. An idea reviewed in Smith and Medin (1981).
3. Especially Wittgenstein (1953) and Rosch (1973).
4. Nosofsky (1992).
5. Hampton (2000); Rosch and Mervis (1975); Smith and Minda (2002).
6. Carey (1985); Keil (1989); Murphy and Medin (1985).
7. See Sloman and Malt (2003).
8. Keil (1989).
9. Rips (2001).
10. See Rehder (2003; Rehder & Hastie, 2001) for a rigorous presentation of this idea.
11. Strevens (2001) shows that causal knowledge is sufficient to explain most of the data on the importance of nonobservables in categorization.
12. Kemler Nelson, Frankenfield, Morris, and Blair (2000). See also Kemler Nelson, Egan, and Holt (2004).
13. See Chaigneau and Barsalou (in press) for a review.
14. Malt and Johnson (1992). For corroborating data, see Sloman, Malt, and Fridman (2001).

15. Chaigneau, Barsalou, and Sloman (2004).
16. See Keil (1995).
17. Rehder (2003) offers a detailed probabilistic model of categorization based on causal relations.
18. See Ross and Murphy (1999).
19. Sloman, Love, and Ahn (1998).
20. Hampton (1982).
21. Brown (1958).
22. Rosch and Mervis (1975).
23. Rehder and Hastie (2004) offer a theory consistent with this idea. Judgments of typicality have multiple determinants that include frequency and similarity to a prototype, as well as consistency with a causal model (Hampton, 1998, offers a detailed analysis).
24. See Malt's (1994) "Water is not H_2O."
25. Lewis (1929). Rips (2001) also discusses the idea in the domain of natural kinds in the guise of what he calls the *interactionist view*: "natural kinds are the sorts of entities that causal laws relate."

10. Categorical Induction

1. Hume (1748).
2. Plumley (1975), pp. 17–41.
3. For a review, see Sloman and Lagnado (2005b).
4. Heit and Rubinstein (1994).
5. Medin, Coley, Storms, and Hayes (2003).
6. Sloman (1994, 1997).
7. Nisbett, Krantz, Jepson, and Kunda (1983).
8. See Hadjichristidis, Sloman, Stevenson, and Over (2004).
9. Sloman, Love, and Ahn (1998).
10. Rehder and Hastie (2001, 2004) present a probabilistic model of induction that's intended to be causal. Kemp and Tenenbaum (2003) offer a related Bayesian approach.

11. Locating Causal Structure in Language

1. The earliest discussions of this phenomenon can be found in Abelson and Kanouse (1966) and Brown and Fish (1983). See Rudolph and Forsterling (1997) for a review.
2. Such effects could in principle be mediated solely by knowledge of linguistic structure with no appeal to causal knowledge. Rudolph and Forsterling (1997) show that the evidence speaks against such a possibility and in favor of Kelley's (1967) covariation principle, that people attribute cause and effect according to patterns of covariation. All the evidence in favor of covariation is correlational, however, and therefore, it's unclear

whether perception of the relevant covariations elicit causal schema of implicit causality in verbs, as Kelley would have it, or whether the causal schema cause the covariations to be perceived, or whether some third variable is responsible for both.

3. See Garnham, Traxler, Oakhill, and Gernsbacher (1996) and Stewart , Pickering, and Sanford (2000).

4. This view is shared by Johnson-Laird and Byrne (2002). A parallel analysis of causal verbs (to cause, to enable, to prevent) can be found in Goldvarg and Johnson-Laird (2001).

5. See Edgington (1995) for a review.

6. Lewis (1973).

7. See Ramsey (1931).

8. The initial publications were Stalnaker (1968) and Lewis (1973).

9. More generally, many of the properties or variables used as examples in this chapter are complex, some relational or expressing implicit temporality. These kinds of structure all pose unsolved representational problems for the causal Bayesian network formalism.

10. See Kaufmann (2004, in press) for a sophisticated discussion of this point.

12. Causal Learning

1. For a review, see Cheng and Buehner (2005).

2. Allan (1980).

3. Danks (2003).

4. E.g., Shanks and Dickinson (1987); Shanks (1995).

5. Cheng (1997). See Novick and Cheng (2004) for more recent developments.

6. Buehner and Cheng, 1997; Lober and Shanks, 2000; Perales and Shanks, 2003.

7. Collins and Shanks (2003).

8. The most developed algorithm of this kind is called TETRAD and is described in Spirtes, Glymour, and Scheines (1993). For a friendlier presentation, see Glymour (2001). Gopnik et al. (2004) offer a psychological analysis.

9. See, e.g., Heckerman, Meek, and Cooper (1999). Articles with a psychological orientation include Griffiths, Baraff, and Tenenbaum (2004) and Tenenbaum and Griffiths (2001).

10. Waldmann (1996).

11. Klayman and Ha (1987).

12. Hagmayer and Waldmann (2002).

13. Cohen, Amsel, Redford, and Casasola (1998).

14. Heider and Simmel (1944).

15. Lagnado and Sloman (2004).

16. Schulz and Gopnik (2004).

17. Lagnado and Sloman (2004); Sobel (2003); Steyvers, Tenenbaum, Wagenmakers, and Blum (2003).

18. Kuhn (2002).

19. Lien and Cheng (2000).

13. Conclusion: Causation in the Mind

1. Much more has been said. Here are a few of the many relevant references: Hart and Honore (1985); Lipton (1992); Nozick (1995); Spellman and Kincannon (2001).

2. I thank David Danks for emphasizing these limitations.

3. Cheng and Holyoak (1985) suggested that human reasoning uses *pragmatic reasoning schema*—bundles of knowledge that embody rules specific to a domain of reasoning that are useful for achieving people's goals. These are a type of module for reasoning. Fodor (1983) discusses the possible roles and characteristics of modules in cognition more generally.

References

Abelson, R. P., & Kanouse, D. E. (1966). Subjective acceptance of verbal generalizations. In S. Feldman (Ed.), *Cognitive consistency: Motivational antecedents and behavioral consequents* (pp. 171–197). New York: Academic Press.

Ajzen, I. (1977). Intuitive theories of events and the effects of base-rate information on prediction. *Journal of Personality and Social Psychology, 35,* 303–314.

Allan, L. G. (1980). A note on measurements of contingency between two binary variables in judgment tasks. *Bulletin of the Psychonomic Society, 15,* 147–149.

Anderson, C. A., Lepper, M. R., & Ross, L. (1980). The perseverance of social theories: The role of explanation in the persistence of discredited information. *Journal of Personality & Social Psychology, 39,* 1037–1049.

Andersson, B. (1986). The experiential gestalt of causation: A common core to pupil's preconceptions in science. *European Journal of Scientific Education, 8,* 155–171.

Arnheim, R. (1969). *Visual thinking.* Berkeley: University of California Press.

Bacon, F. (1620). *The works* (vol. VIII). Translated by J. Spedding, R. L. Ellis, & D. D. Heath (1863). Boston: Taggard and Thompson.

Bartlett, F. C. (1932). *Remembering: A study in experimental and social psychology.* New York: Cambridge University Press.

Biederman, I., & Shiffrar, M. M. (1987). Sexing day-old chicks. *Journal of Experimental Psychology: Learning, Memory, and Cognition, 13,* 640–645.

Brown, R. (1958). How shall a thing be called? *Psychological Review, 65,* 14–21.

Brown, R., & Fish, D. (1983). The psychological causality implicit in language. *Cognition, 14,* 237–273.

Bruner, J. S. (1973). *Beyond the information given: Studies in the psychology of knowing.* New York: Norton.

Buehner, M. J., & Cheng, P. W. (1997). Causal induction: The power PC theory versus the Rescorla-Wagner theory. In M. G. Shafto & P. Langley (Eds.), *Proceedings of the nineteenth annual conference of the Cognitive Science Society* (pp. 55–60). Mahwah, NJ: Erlbaum.

Camerer, C. F. (1995). Individual decision making. In J. Kagel & A. Roth (Eds.), *Handbook of experimental economics.* Princeton: Princeton University Press.

Carey, S. (1985). *Conceptual change in childhood.* Cambridge, MA: MIT Press.

Chaigneau, S. E., & Barsalou, L. W. (in press). The role of function in categorization. *Theoria et Historia Scientiarum.*

Chaigneau, S. E., Barsalou, L. W., & Sloman, S. A. (2004). Assessing affordance and intention in the HIPE theory of function. *Journal of Experimental Psychology: General, 133,* 601–625.

Chapman, L. J., & Chapman, J. P. (1969). Illusory correlation as an obstacle to the use of valid psychodiagnostic signs. *Journal of Abnormal Psychology, 74,* 271–280.

Cheng, P. W. (1997). From covariation to causation: A causal power theory. *Psychological Review, 104,* 367–405.

Cheng, P. W., & Buehner, M. (2005). Causal learning. In R. Morrison & K. Holyoak (Eds.), *Cambridge handbook of thinking & reasoning* (pp. 143–168). Cambridge: Cambridge University Press.

Cheng, P. W., & Holyoak, K. J. (1985). Pragmatic reasoning schemas. *Cognitive Psychology, 17,* 391–416.

Cohen, L. B., Amsel, G., Redford, M. A., & Casasola, M. (1998). The development of infant causal perception. In A. Slator (Ed.), *Perceptual development: Visual, auditory and speech perception in infancy* (pp. 167–209). London: UCL Press and Taylor and Francis.

Collins, D. J., & Shanks, D. R. (2003). *Conformity to the power PC theory of causal induction depends on type of probe question.* Manuscript.

Danks, D. (2003). Equilibria of the Rescorla-Wagner model. *Journal of Mathematical Psychology, 47,* 109–121.

diSessa, A. A. (1993). Towards an epistemology of physics. *Cognition and Instruction, 10,* 105–225.

Dougherty, M. R. P., Gettys, C. F., & Thomas, R. P. (1997). The role of mental simulation in judgments of likelihood. *Organizational Behavior and Human Decision Processes, 70,* 135–148.

Driver, R., Guesne, E., & Tiberghien, A. (1993). Some features of children's ideas and their implications for teaching. In R. Driver, E. Guesne,

&. A. Tiberghien (Eds.), *Children's ideas in science* (pp. 193–201). Buckingham, United Kingdom: Open University.

Edgington, D. (1995). On conditionals. *Mind, 104,* 235–329.

Fischhoff, B., Slovic, P., & Lichtenstein, S. (1978). Fault trees: Sensitivity of estimated failure probabilities to problem representation. *Journal of Experimental Psychology: Human Perception and Performance, 4,* 330–344.

Fodor, J. A. (1983). *The modularity of mind.* Cambridge, MA: MIT Press.

Forbus, K. D. (1984). Qualitative process theory. *Artificial Intelligence, 24,* 85–168.

Forbus, K. D. (1996). Qualitative reasoning. A. B. Tucker (Ed.), In *The computer science and engineering handbook* (pp. 715–733). Boca Raton, FL: CRC.

Garnham, A., Traxler, M., Oakhill, J. V., & Gernsbacher, M. A. (1996). The locus of implicit causality effects in comprehension. *Journal of Memory and Language, 35,* 517–543.

Gentner, D., & Stevens, A. (1983). (Eds.). *Mental models.* Hillsdale, NJ: Erlbaum.

Gibson, J. J. (1979). *The ecological approach to visual perception.* Boston: Houghton Mifflin.

Gilovich, T., Vallone, R., & Tversky, A. (1985). The hot hand in basketball: On the misperception of random sequences. *Cognitive Psychology, 17,* 295–314.

Gillies, D. (2001). *Philosophical theories of probability.* London: Routledge.

Glymour, C. (2001). *The mind's arrows.* Cambridge, MA: MIT Press.

Goldvarg, Y., & Johnson-Laird, P. N. (2001). Naïve causality: A mental model theory of causal meaning and reasoning. *Cognitive Science, 25,* 565–610.

Gopnik, A., Glymour, C., Sobel, D. M., Schulz, L. E., Kushnir, T., & Danks, D. (2004). A theory of causal learning in children: Causal maps and Bayes nets. *Psychological Review, 111,* 3–32.

Griffiths, T. L., Baraff, E. R., & Tenenbaum, J. B. (2004). Using physical theories to infer hidden causal structure. *Proceedings of the Twenty-Sixth Annual Conference of the Cognitive Science Society,* 500–505.

Hacking, I. (2001). *An introduction to probability and logic.* Cambridge: Cambridge University Press.

Hadjichristidis, C., Sloman, S. A., Stevenson, R. J., & Over, D. E. (2004). Feature centrality and property induction. *Cognitive Science, 28,* 45–74.

Hagmayer, Y., & Waldmann, M. R. (2002). How temporal assumptions influence causal judgments. *Memory & Cognition, 30,* 1128–1137.

Halpern, J. (2003). *Reasoning about uncertainty.* Cambridge, MA: MIT Press.

Halpern, J. Y., & Pearl, J. (2001). Causes and explanations: A structural-model approach. Part I: Causes. In *Proceedings of the Seventeenth*

Conference on Uncertainty in Artificial Intelligence (pp. 194–202). San Francisco, CA: Morgan Kaufmann.

Hampton, J. A. (1982). A demonstration of intransitivity in natural categories. *Cognition, 12,* 151–164.

Hampton, J. A. (1998). Similarity-based categorization and fuzziness of natural categories. In S. A. Sloman & L. J. Rips (Eds.), *Similarity and symbols in human thinking* (pp. 51–79). Cambridge, MA: MIT Press.

Hampton, J. A. (2000). Concepts and prototypes. *Mind and Language, 15,* 299–307.

Harman, G. (1995). Rationality. In E. E. Smith & D. N. Osherson (Eds.), *Thinking (An invitation to cognitive science, Vol. 3),* pp. 175–211. Cambridge, MA: MIT Press.

Hart, H. L. A., & Honoré, T. (1985). Causation in the law (2nd ed.). Oxford: Clarendon.

Heckerman, D., Meek, C., & Cooper, G. (1999). A Bayesian approach to causal discovery. In C. Glymour & G. Cooper (Eds.), *Computation, causation, discovery* (pp. 141–165). Cambridge, MA: MIT Press.

Heider, F., & Simmel, M. (1944). An experimental study of apparent behavior. *American Journal of Psychology, 57,* 243–259.

Heit, E., & Rubinstein, J. (1994). Similarity and property effects in inductive reasoning. *Journal of Experimental Psychology: Learning, Memory, and Cognition, 20,* 411–422.

Hitchcock, C. (2001). The intransitivity of causation revealed in equations and graphs. *Journal of Philosophy, 98,* 273–299.

Hoffman, C., & Tchir, M. A. (1990). Interpersonal verbs and dispositional adjectives: The psychology of causality embodied in language. *Journal of Personality and Social Psychology, 58,* 765–778.

Howard, R., & Matheson, J. (1981). Influence diagrams. In R. Howard, & J. Matheson (Eds.), *Readings on the principles and applications of decision analysis,* Volume 2 (pp. 721–762). Menlo Park, CA: Strategic Decisions Group.

Hoyle, F. (1957). *The black cloud.* London: Heinemann.

Hume, D. (1748). *An enquiry concerning human understanding.* Oxford: Clarendon.

Hunt, E., & Minstrell, J. (1994). A cognitive approach to the teaching of physics. In K. McGilly (Ed.), *Classroom lessons: Integrating cognitive theory and classroom practice* (pp. 51–74). Cambridge, MA: MIT Press.

Johnson-Laird, P. N., & Byrne, R. M. J. (1991). *Deduction.* Hillsdale, NJ: Erlbaum.

Johnson-Laird, P. N., & Byrne, R. M. J. (2002). Conditionals: A theory of meaning, pragmatics, and inference. *Psychological Review, 109,* 646–678.

Jones, E. E., & Harris, V. A. (1967). The attribution of attitudes. *Journal of Experimental Social Psychology, 3,* 1–24.

Kahneman, D., & Frederick, S. (2002). Representativeness revisited: Attribute substitution in intuitive judgment. In T. Gilovich, D.

Griffin, & D. Kahneman (Eds.), *Heuristics & biases: The psychology of intuitive judgment* (pp. 49–81). New York: Cambridge University Press.

Kahneman, D., & Tversky, A. (1982). The simulation heuristic. In D. Kahneman, P. Slovic, & A. Tversky (Eds.), *Judgement under uncertainty: Heuristics and biases* (pp. 201–210). Cambridge, MA: Cambridge University Press.

Kaufmann, S. (2004). Conditioning against the grain: Abduction and indicative conditionals. *Journal of Philosophical Logic, 33,* 583–606.

Kaufmann, S. (in press). Conditional predictions: A probabilistic account. *Linguistics and Philosophy.*

Keil, F. C. (1989). *Concepts, kinds, and cognitive development.* Cambridge, MA: MIT Press.

Keil, F. C. (1995). The growth of causal understanding of natural kinds. In D. Sperber, D. Premack, & A. J. Premack (Eds.), *Causal cognition: A multidisciplinary approach* (pp. 234–262). New York: Oxford University Press.

Keil, F. C. (2003). Folkscience: Coarse interpretations of a complex reality. *Trends in Cognitive Science, 7,* 368–373.

Kelley, H. H. (1967). Attribution theory in social psychology. In D. Levine (Ed.), *Nebraska symposium on motivation, 15* (pp. 192–238). Lincoln: University of Nebraska Press.

Kemler Nelson, D. G., Egan, L. C.; & Holt, M. B. (2004). When children ask, "what is it?" what do they want to know about artifacts? *Psychological Science, 15,* 384–389.

Kemler Nelson, D. G., Frankenfield, A., Morris, C., & Blair, E. (2000). Young children's use of functional information to categorize artifacts: Three factors that matter. *Cognition, 77,* 133–168.

Kemp, C., & Tenenbaum, J. B. (2003). Theory-based induction. *Proceedings of the Twenty-Fifth Annual Conference of the Cognitive Science Society,* Boston, MA.

Keren, G., & Wagenaar, W. A. (1985). On the psychology of playing Blackjack. Normative and descriptive considerations with implications for decision theory. *Journal of Experimental Psychology: General, 114,* 133–158.

Klayman, J., & Ha, Y. (1987). Confirmation, disconfirmation, and information in hypothesis testing. *Psychological Review, 94,* 211–28.

Kuhn, D. (2002). What is scientific thinking and how does it develop? In U. Goswami (Ed.), (pp. 371–393). *Handbook of childhood cognitive development.* Oxford: Blackwell.

Lagnado, D., & Sloman, S. A. (2004). The advantage of timely intervention. *Journal of Experimental Psychology: Learning, Memory, and Cognition, 30,* 856–876.

Larkin, J. (1983). The role of problem representation in physics. In D. Gentner & A. Stevens (Eds.), *Mental models.* (pp. 75–98). Hillsdale, NJ: Erlbaum.

Lewis, C. I. (1929/1956). Mind and the world order: An outline of a theory of knowledge. New York: Charles Scribner's Sons, reprinted in paperback by Dover Publications, Inc.

Lewis, D. (1973). *Counterfactuals.* Oxford: Basil Blackwell.

Lewis, D. (1976). Probabilities of conditionals and conditional probabilities. *Philosophical Review, 85,* 297–315.

Lewis, D. (1986). *Philosophical papers.* Vol. 2. New York: Oxford University Press.

Lien, Y., & Cheng, P. W. (2000). Distinguishing genuine from spurious causes: A coherence hypothesis. *Cognitive Psychology, 40,* 87–137.

Lipton, P. (1992). Causation outside the law. In H. Gross & R. Harrison (Eds.), *Jurisprudence: Cambridge essays.* Oxford: Oxford University Press.

Lober, K., & Shanks, D. R. (2000). Is causal induction based on causal power? Critique of Cheng (1997). *Psychological Review, 107,* 195–212.

Luria, A. R. (1968). *The mind of a mnemonist: A little book about a vast memory.* Translated by L. Solotaroff. Cambridge, MA: Harvard University Press.

Mackie, J. L. (1980). *The cement of the universe: A study of causation.* Oxford: Clarendon.

Malt, B. C. (1994). Water is not H_2O. *Cognitive Psychology, 27,* 41–70.

Malt, B. C., & Johnson, E. J. (1992). Do artifact concepts have cores? *Journal of Memory and Language, 31,* 195–217.

Mandel, D. R. (2003). Judgment dissociation theory: An analysis of differences in causal, counterfactual, and covariational reasoning. *Journal of Experimental Psychology: General, 132,* 419–434.

Medin, D. L., Coley, J. D., Storms, G., & Hayes, B. (2003). A relevance theory of induction. *Psychonomic Bulletin and Review, 10,* 517–532.

Meek, C., & Glymour, C. (1994). Conditioning and intervening. *British Journal for the Philosophy of Science, 45,* 1001–1021.

Michotte, A. (1946/1963). *La perception de la causalité.* Louvain: Institut supérieur de la Philosophie, English translation. by T. R. Miles. The perception of causality. London: Methuen.

Mochon, D., & Sloman, S. A. (2004). Causal models frame interpretation of mathematical equations. *Psychonomic Bulletin & Review, 11,* 1099–1104.

Morris, M. W., & Larrick, R. (1995). When one cause casts doubt on another: A normative analysis of discounting in causal attribution. *Psychological Review, 102,* 331–355.

Murphy, G. L., & Medin, D. L. (1985). The role of theories in conceptual coherence. *Psychological Review, 92,* 289–316.

Nisbett, R. E., Krantz, D. H., Jepson, D. H., & Kunda, Z. (1983). The use of statistical heuristics in everyday inductive reasoning. *Psychological Review, 90,* 339–363.

Novick, L. R., & Cheng, P. W. (2004). Assessing interactive causal influence. *Psychological Review, 111,* 455–485.

Nosofsky, R. M. (1992). Exemplar-based approach to relating categorization, identification, and recognition. In F. G. Ashby (Ed.), *Multidimensional models of perception and cognition* (pp. 363–393). Hillsdale, NJ: Erlbaum.

Nozick, R. (1969). Newcomb's problem and two principles of choice. In N. Rescher (Ed.), *Essays in honor of Carl G. Hempel* (pp. 107–133). Dordrecht, Holland: Reidel.

Nozick, R. (1995). *The nature of rationality.* Princeton: Princeton University Press.

Pearl, J. (1988). *Probabilistic reasoning in intelligent systems.* San Fransisco, CA: Morgan Kaufmann.

Pearl, J. (2000). *Causality: Models, reasoning and inference.* New York: Cambridge University Press.

Pennington, N., & Hastie, R. (1993). Reasoning in explanation-based decision making. *Cognition, 49,* 123–163.

Perales, J. C., & Shanks, D. R. (2003). Normative and descriptive accounts of the influence of power and contingency on causal judgment. *Quarterly Journal of Experimental Psychology, 56A,* 977–1007.

Plumley, J. M. (1975). The cosmology of ancient Egypt. In C. Blacker & M. Loewe (Eds.), *Ancient cosmologies* (pp. 17–41). London: George Allen & Unwin Ltd.

Quattrone, G., & Tversky A. (1984). Causal versus diagnostic contingencies: On self-deception and on the voter's illusion. *Journal of Personality and Social Psychology, 46,* 237–248.

Quattrone, G., & Tversky, A. (1988). Contrasting rational and psychological analyses of political choice. *American Political Science Review, 82,* 719–736.

Ramsey, F. P. (1931). *The foundations of mathematics and other logical essays.* R. B. Braithwaite (Ed.). New York: Routledge and Kegan Paul.

Rehder, B. (2003). A causal-model theory of conceptual representation and categorization. *Journal of Experimental Psychology: Learning, Memory, and Cognition , 29,* 1141–1159.

Rehder, B., & Hastie, R. (2001). Causal knowledge and categories: The effects of causal beliefs on categorization, induction, and similarity. *Journal of Experimental Psychology: General, 130,* 323–360.

Rehder, B., & Hastie, R. (2004). Category coherence and category-based property induction. *Cognition, 91,* 113–153.

Reif, F., & Allen, S. (1992). Cognition for interpreting scientific concepts: A study of acceleration. *Cognition and Instruction, 9,* 1–44.

Reiner, M., Slotta, J. D., Chi, M. T. H., & Resnick, L. B. (2000). Naïve physics reasoning: A commitment to substance-based conceptions. *Cognition and Instruction, 18,* 1–34.

Rescorla, R. A., & Wagner, A. R. (1972). A theory of Pavlovian conditioning: Variations in the effectiveness of reinforcement and nonreinforcement. In A. H. Black & W. F. Prokasy (Eds.), *Classical conditioning II: Current theory and research* (pp. 64–99). New York: Appleton-Century-Crofts.

Rips, L. (2001). Necessity and natural categories. *Psychological Bulletin, 127*, 827–852.

Rosch, E. (1973). On the internal structure of perceptual and semantic categories. In T. E. Moore (Ed.), *Cognitive development and the acquisition of language* (pp. 111–144). New York: Academic Press.

Rosch, E., & Mervis, C. B. (1975). Family resemblances: Studies in the internal structure of categories. *Cognitive Psychology, 7*, 573–605.

Ross, B. H., & Murphy, G. L. (1999). Food for thought: Cross-classification and category organization in a complex real-world domain. *Cognitive Psychology, 38*, 495–553.

Ross, L., & Anderson, C. A. (1982). Shortcomings in the attribution process: On the origins and maintenance of erroneous social assessments. In D. Kahneman, P. Slovic, & A. Tversky (Eds.), *Judgment under uncertainty: Heuristics and biases.* Cambridge: Cambridge University Press.

Rudolph, U., & Forsterling, F. (1997). The psychological causality implicit in verbs: A review. *Psychological Bulletin, 121*, 192–218.

Russell, B. (1913). On the notion of cause. *Proceedings of the Aristotelian Society, 13*, 1–26.

Russell, B. (1948). *Human knowledge: Its scope and limits.* New York: Simon and Schuster.

Schulz, L. E., & Gopnik, A. (2004). Causal learning across domains. *Developmental Psychology, 40*, 162–176.

Shafer, G. (1996). *The art of causal conjecture.* Cambridge, MA: MIT Press.

Shanks, D. R. (1995). *The psychology of associative learning.* Cambridge: Cambridge University Press.

Shanks, D. R., & Dickinson, A. (1987). Associative accounts of causality judgment. In G. H. Bower (Ed.), *The psychology of learning and motivation: Advances in research and theory, 21* (pp. 229–261). San Diego, CA: Academic Press.

Sherin, B. L. (2001). How students understand physics equations. *Cognition and Instruction, 19*, 479–541.

Sloman, S. A. (1994). When explanations compete: The role of explanatory coherence on judgments of likelihood. *Cognition, 52*, 1–21.

Sloman, S. A. (1997). Explanatory coherence and the induction of properties. *Thinking and Reasoning, 3*, 81–110.

Sloman, S. A. (1998). Categorical inference is not a tree: The myth of inheritance hierarchies. *Cognitive Psychology, 35*, 1–33.

Sloman, S. A., & Lagnado, D. (2005a). Do we "do"? *Cognitive Science, 29*, 5–39.

Sloman, S. A., & Lagnado, D. (2005b). The problem of induction. In R. Morrison and K. Holyoak (Eds.), *Cambridge handbook of thinking & reasoning* (pp. 95–116). Cambridge: Cambridge University Press.

Sloman, S. A., Love, B. C., & Ahn, W. (1998). Feature centrality and conceptual coherence. *Cognitive Science, 22*, 189–228.

Sloman, S. A., & Malt, B. C. (2003). Artifacts are not ascribed essences, nor are they treated as belonging to kinds. *Language and Cognitive Processes, 18,* 563–582.

Sloman, S. A., Malt, B. C., & Fridman, A. (2001). Categorization versus similarity: The case of container names. In M. Ramscar, U. Hahn, E. Cambouropolos, & H. Pain (Eds.), *Similarity and categorization* (pp. 73–86). Cambridge: Cambridge University Press.

Smith, E. E., & Medin, D. L. (1981). *Categories and concepts.* Cambridge, MA: Harvard University Press.

Smith, J. D., & Minda, J. P. (2002). Distinguishing prototype-based and exemplar-based processes in category learning. *Journal of Experimental Psychology: Learning, Memory, and Cognition, 28,* 800–811.

Sobel, D. (2003). *Watch it, do it, or watch it done.* Manuscript submitted for publication.

Spellman, B. A., & Kincannon, A. (2001). The relation between counter-factual ("but for") and causal reasoning: Experimental findings and implications for jurors' decisions. *Law and Contemporary Problems: Causation in Law and Science, 64,* 241–264.

Spirtes, P., Glymour, C., & Scheines, R. (1993). *Causation, prediction, and search.* New York: Springer-Verlag.

Stalnaker, R. C. (1968). A theory of conditionals. In N. Rescher (Ed.), *Studies in Logical Theory, American Philosophical Quarterly* monograph series, pp. 98–112. Oxford: Blackwell.

Stewart, A. J., Pickering, M. J., & Sanford, A. J. (2000). The time course of the influence of implicit causality information: Focusing versus integration accounts. *Journal of Memory and Language, 42,* 423–443.

Steyvers, M., Tenenbaum, J. B., Wagenmakers, E. J., & Blum, B. (2003). Inferring causal networks from observations and interventions. *Cognitive Science, 27,* 453–489.

Stich, S. (1990). *The fragmentation of reason.* Cambridge, MA: MIT Press.

Strevens, M. (2001). The essentialist aspect of naive theories. *Cognition, 74,* 149–175.

Tenenbaum, J. B., & Griffiths, T. L. (2001). Structure learning in human causal induction. In T. K. Leen, T. G. Dietterich, & V. Tresp (Eds.), *Advances in Neural Information Processing Systems, 13,* (pp. 59–65). Cambridge, MA: MIT Press.

Turing, A. M. (1950). Computing machinery and intelligence. *Mind, 59,* 433–460.Tversky, A., & Kahneman, D. (1980). Causal schemas in judgments under uncertainty. In M. Fishbein (Ed.), *Progress in social psychology.* Hillsdale, NJ: Lawrence Erlbaum. Partially reproduced in Kahneman, D., Slovic, P., & Tversky, A. (1982). *Judgment under uncertainty: Heuristics and biases.* Cambridge: Cambridge University Press.

Tversky, A., & Kahneman, D. (1982). Evidential impact of base rates. In D. Kahneman, P. Slovic, & A. Tversky (Eds.), *Judgment under uncertainty: Heuristics and biases,* (pp. 153–160). Cambridge: Cambridge University Press.

Tversky, A., & Kahneman, D. (1983). Extensional versus intuitive reasoning: The conjunction fallacy in probability judgement. *Psychological Review, 90,* 293–315.

Vallée-Tourangeau, F., Murphy, R. A., Drew, S., & Baker, A. G. (1998). Judging the importance of constant and variable candidate causes: A test of the Power PC theory. *Quarterly Journal of Experimental Psychology, 51A,* 65–84.

Waldmann, M. R. (1996). Knowledge-based causal induction. In D. R. Shanks, K. J. Holyoak, & D. L. Medin (Eds.), *The psychology of learning and motivation, Vol. 34: Causal learning* (pp. 47–88). San Diego: Academic Press.

Wells, G. L. (1992). Naked statistical evidence of liability: Is subjective probability enough? *Journal of Personality and Social Psychology, 62,* 739–752.

Wittgenstein, L. (1953). *Philosophical investigations.* New York: Macmillan.

Woodward, J. (2003). *Making things happen: A theory of causal explanation.* New York: Oxford University Press.

Index

Abstract models, 129–30
Accidents, 111–14, 113*f*–114*f*, 175
Actions
  agent, 122–24
  causality and, 20, 52
  cognition for, 176–78
  imagination and, 78
  as intervention, 57–63, 84
  judgments and, 19, 115
  observation *v.*, 52–66, 151
Agency, 3–8, 5–6, 181
Agent intention/action, 122–24
Airplanes, 116, 125–27, 126*f*
Airports, traffic jams and, 105–6
Ajzen, I., 112
Algorithms, 160, 188*n*8
Analogy, 140, 155, 164
And, 141, 142–43
Animals. *See also specific animals*
  categorization of, 119–20, 128–31
  causal models of, 120, 126–27,
    126*f*, 130
  induction and, 134–37, 135*f*–137*f*
  learning and, 155, 168
  properties of, 134–37
Aristotle, 183*n*1, 185*n*17

Artifacts, 118, 122–24, 122*f*, 125*f*,
  139
Artificial intelligence, 49, 82
Associations, 25, 32
Associative learning, 155, 157–59,
  167–68
Assumptions, 47–49, 60–61, 106,
  160, 165, 176

Backdoor paths, 62
Bacon, Francis, 23
Bacterial infection, peptic ulcer *v.*,
  54–62, 57*f*–58*f*, 62*f*
Balls, 116–17, 166
Barsalou, Larry, 122, 124
Bartlett, Sir Frederick, 88
Base rates, 112–14, 113*f*–114*f*, 159
Bayes' rule, 53–57, 59, 162
Bayes, Thomas, 53
Bayesian networks, 179
  on cab accident, 111–12, 113,
    114*f*
  formalism, 175, 188*n*9
  on induction, 187*n*10
  on learning, 160, 162–63
  probability and, 7, 36, 184*n*2